Picture It!

How God can
artistic gifts

by PAUL CLOWNEY

A Bible Society Creative Handbook

For churches, teachers, and youth leaders

BIBLE SOCIETY
Stonehill Green, Westlea, Swindon SN5 7DG, England

Unless otherwise stated, quotations from the Bible are from the Good News
Bible, published by the Bible Societies/Collins, © American Bible Society,
New York, 1966, 1971, 1976.

First published 1987

British Library Cataloguing in Publication Data
Clowney, Paul
Picture it! : how God can use your
artistic gifts.—(Creative handbooks).
1. Art—Technique 2. Art and religion
I. Title II. Bible Society III. Series
702'.8 N7430.5
ISBN 0–564–07792–5

Acknowledgements: Page 87 (bottom) reprinted by permission
of The Times © Times Newspaper Ltd; (top) reprinted by permission of BMW

Printed in Great Britain by Stanley L. Hunt (Printers) Ltd,
Midland Road, Rushden, Northants.

Bible Societies exist to provide resources for Bible distribution and use.
Bible Society in England and Wales (BFBS) is a member of the United Bible
Societies, an international partnership working in over 180 countries. Their
common aim is to reach all people with the Bible, or some part of it, in a
language they can understand and at a price they can afford. Parts of the
Bible have now been translated into approximately 1,800 languages. Bible
Societies aim to help every church at every point where it uses the Bible. You
are invited to share in this work by your prayers and gifts. Bible Society in
your country will be very happy to provide details of its activity.

Contents

Sketches/Notes

Foreword

For many centuries the Church has encouraged different forms of musical expression. For hundreds of years it has made use of the printed word. And in the last few decades other mediums for worship have been discovered (or rediscovered), for example dance, drama, and creative writing. The visual arts, however, have lain dormant for far too long.

Granted there have been visual artists glorifying God through their skills from the days of the early church. But all too often it has been the **professional** draughtsman, the **skilled** stonemason, the **renowned** painter, who alone has been employed.

At last Paul Clowney has written a book that seeks to release a dormant gift or gifts that could lie within many of us. In this expansive volume he liberates the artist in the pew. School-day inhibitions about being "unable to draw a straight line" are brushed aside, and with warmth and enthusiasm Paul Clowney encourages the reader to "have a go" at a whole range of visual art forms.

Reading this book is fun and rewarding. A deep and thoughtful theme runs through the text which should lead the reader to experience anew the wonder of God and his gifts.

TAFFY DAVIES

"I think I might have been a bit too enthusiastic about Paul Clowney's book last week!"

Introduction

Close your eyes and imagine that you couldn't open them again. How would your life change? How would you get around, eat, work, or read? How many times would you hear someone say, "Look at . . ." and then stop abruptly?

Now imagine the excitement of rediscovering sight:

Jesus Heals a Blind Man at Bethsaida

²² They came to Bethsaida, where some people brought a blind man to Jesus and begged him to touch him. ²³Jesus took the blind man by the hand and led him out of the village. After spitting on the man's eyes, Jesus placed his hands on him and asked him, "Can you see anything?"

²⁴ The man looked up and said, "Yes, I can see people, but they look like trees walking about."

²⁵ Jesus again placed his hands on the man's eyes. This time the man looked intently, his eyesight returned, and he saw everything clearly. ²⁶Jesus then sent him home with the order, "Don't go back into the village."

(Mark 8.22–26)

When Jesus healed the blind man the fortunate fellow felt the windows open on his world. His comment as he receives the first glimpse of the world, "I can see people, but they look like trees walking about", touches us by its simplicity and innocence. For when it comes to seeing we are very skilled indeed.

Our eyes are extraordinarily complex. In the high-technology world of computers and robotics, huge sums are being spent to develop machines that can "see". These combinations of lenses, hydraulics, and electronics can now sort components on an assembly line or recognize an aircraft from different profiles. But what a poor cousin they are to real eyes! They can't blink with astonishment, take in a whole scene at a glance, or consider the stars.

Seeing is not just an act of recording or registering. It is also an act of interpreting. Three people may be present in the same room but see entirely different things, because what is seen depends not only on what is there. It also depends on who is doing the seeing, and how they interpret what they see.

Try this out for yourself using the following exercise. Look at the ink-blot illustration for thirty seconds. What do you see?

What can you see in this design?

Now if there's a friend around, or you don't mind embarrassing your neighbours on the train, pass it to them. Ask them what they see.

Finally, look again yourself. Did you see the same? Has their perception changed what you can see?

Actually there's nothing "there". Or to be more accurate, there's nothing there by design. The shape is accidental. Yet the mind is always searching for images and will find a similarity to something in any pattern. The mind will add new meanings to whatever the eye sees. This is one of the things that gives the language of pictures and images its great power. But it also follows that no matter how precisely a picture is painted it will always be a bit unpredictable. It probably won't mean the same thing to you as it does to me. And yet we still use the phrase "get the picture", because with the right context a picture can make everything clear.

Picture It! is about the use of images in exploring the Bible and in expressing the richness of the Christian faith. It is for anyone who likes pictures. You don't have to be "artistic", just interested. And if you are only marginally interested, the book aims to make you properly interested.

The first thought which comes to mind when putting pictures together with the Bible is probably of "picture Bibles" — that massive old family Bible with pressed-flower stains alternating with engraved illustrations, or one of the modern editions with colour photos of the Bible lands. But think again. What is the Bible about? What images come to mind when you think about the Christian life or the fruits of the Spirit? How could a picture be made to convey the notion of forgiveness?

Picture It! describes a series of tools which can help bring God's Word to life in your personal and group expression. With some thought, practice, and encouragement anyone able to hold a pencil can find a limitless source of ideas for creative expression in the Bible.

The chief tool is our imagination. The gift of imagination can't be better used than if we use it to "imagine" God. Imagine how Jesus would respond, imagine how he sees us, imagine the application of his teaching. This book tries to foster imaginative growth and a sense of wonder at the fact that we are the product of his imagination. It has hints and reflections on Bible exploration and practical ideas for many art forms. As you read you will come up with many ideas of your own which you may like to scribble in the margins.

Many people have somehow developed the idea that they are not creative. In a way they are right. In the true sense no one but God is creative. Only God can create from nothing. The rest of us just shuffle the bits he has already created. To be sure, some are particularly good at it, and others less so. But our opinions and self-imposed limitations require reassessment. I would guess that you are probably more capable of inventive thinking and doing than you suspect!

Studies of creative thinking show that in order to be creative people need to feel comfortable and must be willing to experiment.

1. Take it easy

Threat arises in many forms — feeling that one's skills are not up to the task; being pressured to work too quickly; or feeling that others will not approve of our efforts. We can even threaten ourselves by setting impossibly high goals for our work. As Christians we are told that we are not to be "anxious", but we often are. One prerequisite for creativity is that we must relax.

2. Take chances

The ability to experiment may not come easily either, but it can be cultivated. Many people want to engage in crafts and the arts, but quickly get stuck because they can't think of anything to make. Ready-made DIY projects can help get the mind ticking, but there are other ways. Games are good. Items from the world's store of objects, ideas, and environments can be juxtaposed artificially. If you combine a bicycle and a blizzard what do you get? Our minds have wonderful sensitivity to allusion, and such a combination quickly becomes a kernel for a story. A random combination of elements is presented and we immediately set about trying to impose some kind of order. The drawing games in chapter 2 take this theme further. To foster experiment we sometimes have to suppress the desire to reject the unfamiliar, and actually encourage it.

3. Take time

Good ideas sometimes seem to come out of the blue. More often they do not. If there is any kind of pattern it is usually that good ideas come after a period of concentration. You think hard about a problem and then are distracted or give up in frustration. Half-an-hour later, as you are climbing out of the bath — bang — a solution comes to you. The crucial element in this sequence is the period of concentration.

The projects in the book cover quite a broad range, and almost all of them can be done by people with no artistic experience.

The main thing is to relax and enjoy yourself. The benefits of using this book will be both personal and communal. Exploring the Bible and developing an imaginative approach will make you more alert and sensitive, as a Christian and artistically. If you show your work to others (and you should) they will also be spurred to see the Bible anew. Working together in a group will add other benefits. I only regret that I probably won't be able to see the results of your efforts. There are some very good ideas lurking out there!

PAUL CLOWNEY

How to use this book

Who is it for?

Picture It! is not only for artists and church publicists, but for anyone who is interested in using art to explore and express the Bible. In particular, there are activities and projects in here to help:

■ **Youth leaders** looking for ideas for their programme

■ **Church publicists** wishing to improve their churches' publicity

■ **Speakers** or **teachers** wanting to make better use of visual aids

■ **Ministers** wanting to promote a sense of community within their churches

■ **Individuals** wanting to rediscover long-neglected artistic skills and interests

■ **Sunday-school teachers** or **holiday-club leaders** looking for new ideas and teaching methods in children's work

There is an index on page 120 which lists all the projects, and shows for whom they are most useful.

What does the book contain?

There are six chapters. Chapter 1 introduces ideas about how the creative process applies to Bible study and church life. Although it is possible to skip around the book, this chapter should be read first. It will help you to get the most out of the Bible study it contains.

Chapters 2–6 are more or less self-contained units.

Chapter 2 introduces drawing games which will take some of the fear and tension out of artistic experiment. Most you can use on your own. A couple could be used in a group. They are a useful warm-up for all the other activities in *Picture It!*

Chapter 3 describes ways of using visual aids to bring the Bible to life in talks and sermons.

Chapter 4 looks at other visual forms for use in church life — slide-shows, banners, and murals which communicate biblical themes, and which help others to worship God.

Chapter 5 looks at Christian publicity and challenges you to use words and pictures to attract people to the Gospel.

Chapter 6 centres on art as a social and learning activity — applicable to the many groups that make up a typical church. It outlines ways to enjoy art in the company of others. Group activities cement old friendships and facilitate new ones, as well as allowing for many discoveries in Bible study.

Special features

Dotted throughout this book you will find four types of feature:

Worked example... — which give an A-Z description of a project, from the first Bible exploration to the final camera-ready artwork or finished banner. These principles can then be applied to any project.

Technical tips... — which cover a wealth of practical subjects such as "how to prepare artwork for a printer", or "the do's and don'ts of drawing". These tips are also indexed at the back of the book for easy reference.

Try it out... — which suggests projects for you to experiment with. These usually explore particular Bible themes.

■ Boxes

Every now and then some copy is boxed, like this. These boxes further develop ideas mentioned in the text.

What you will need

■ A sketchbook or notebook, to jot down any ideas that come to you as you read — there are also pages at the back of the book for this purpose.

■ A Bible. There are many Bible passages referred to. Take a few moments and look them up, for above all this book aims to get you searching the Bible for yourself. Elsewhere when Bible text is included it is taken from the *Good News Bible*. If you are used to another version, it will be useful to have that alongside you as well.

Picture It! is a guide. There are enough sights and routes to follow for a long time. But the book also tries to push you off the edge of the map. To do your own Bible study and to explore your own imagination. A guide can only direct attention to the things the author knows and has seen. Every author has limitations. Except one. The author of the universe and guide to every twitch of life.

Picture It! points you to that guide, too.

1. The "artist" and the Bible

This short introductory chapter focuses on three basic questions facing those who approach the Bible as "artists":

■ How is the artist seen within the Bible?

■ What can the artist learn from the Bible about how to communicate?

■ How can the artist explore the Bible itself?

How is the artist seen within the Bible?

God is "the artist", in that all of nature is God's creation. His creation shows us something of what he is like. It certainly shows what a visual imagination he has! And as it pleases us to see and enjoy his creation we know that it pleased God, too. We read in Genesis "God looked at everything he had made, and he was very pleased" Genesis 1.31.

What's more, Genesis also describes how human beings were created in God's image. He created us so like himself that we too are creative. So it might surprise us to discover that the artist does not always get a good press in the Bible. Why is this?

One important part of the answer is to be found in the religious practice of Israel's neighbours. The nations surrounding Israel in the time of the Old Testament each had their idols. God, on the other hand, expressly forbade his people to make or worship idols. He deliberately never gave them an official portrait of himself! His people knew that as the source of all things God could not be reduced to an image made of paints, wood, or stone. God is beyond physical appearance. So as you look through passages such as Exodus 20.4, Isaiah 46.5–7, and Hosea 13.2, you will see that rather than *the artist* being condemned, it is the use of the artist's skills to make idols that is under attack.

Nowadays, as the box on page 3 suggests, artists no longer devote much of their energy to religious themes. By implication we might also think, therefore, that the temptation to use our skills to create idols is a thing of the past. But then we tend to think of an idol as a religious figure in the centre of a temple. But an idol surely can be anything which receives the worship which is really due to God — be it a motor car, a home, or even clothes. The negative biblical warning to artists is still relevant.

The positive use of God's gift of art, on the other hand, is to praise God and enjoy him, and direct others to him. Through the arts we can become more aware of God's character and point others towards him. The Bible can assist us in our attempts to communicate. Which leads us to the second question.

What can the artist learn from the Bible about how to communicate?

We'll have a head start in our efforts to communicate the Bible if we understand how the Bible itself communicates with us.

One important tool for all writers, Bible writers included, is "metaphor". At the simplest level a metaphor is a figure of speech in which a word normally used in one sphere of thought is used in another, forcing us to see similarities. Metaphor helps keep language fresh. It changes the context of things so that we see them anew.

For example, when we hear Jesus described as the Lamb of God (John 1.29) what we know about sacrificial lambs, plus what we know about the meekness and innocence of the animal, is said to be true about Jesus. We bring the two spheres of thought together and understand more about Jesus.

A close relation to the metaphor is the "simile", which compares two things, linking them with the words "as" or "like". In Isaiah, for example, God promises his people: "You will be like a child that is nursed by its mother, carried in her arms, and treated with love. I will comfort you in Jerusalem, as a mother comforts her child" (Isaiah 66.12–13). Or in the Sermon on the Mount Jesus encourages his followers: "You are like salt for all mankind . . . You are like light for the whole world" (Matthew 5.13–14).

We all use metaphors and similes in our everyday communication — but often they are metaphors that have been used so often before that no one is surprised to hear them. Take cats, for instance. Think of all the idioms and phrases we use with cats in them: raining cats and dogs, a fat cat, play cat and mouse, when the cat's away . . ., contented as a cat, fight like cats, catty. Yet we rarely ponder felines when we hear these phrases because the metaphoric content has become stale.

Religious art

For centuries the biggest patron of the arts was the church. Murals, paintings, tapestries, sculpture, architecture, illustrated manuscripts, and furniture were made to express the glory of God. Often, however, these things were used to consolidate the political position of the church, or to demonstrate its wealth. As the abuses of the church contributed to its downfall in the political sphere, the rising merchant class replaced it as the most important patron of the arts. The requirements of this class did not eradicate religious themes, for many of the new wealthy traders were anxious either to atone for their dealings or to show their piety.

Gradually, though, a secular ideal prevailed, and by the nineteenth century religious themes were in decline. The religious painting of the nineteenth century generally doesn't appeal to modern taste, as it tends to be sentimental and moralistic.

In the twentieth century there are few artists who regularly treat traditional religious subject matter. The spiritual content still exists, but often in a private mystical form. The interest in historical Christianity in many Western countries is at a low ebb. Examples of artworks with a confessional content are few and far between. This may be due in part to Christian artists recognizing that they need not *only* address the issue of faith in their work. Affirmation of the glories of God's world and man's condition are also important and rewarding themes. Other Christian artists are glad to be free from the ghosts of nineteenth century religious art and wouldn't contemplate treating religious themes.

"Confessional" art is personal by nature, and may use symbols and themes which are obscure. Thus the "religious" character of such expression is difficult to judge. There is no reason that a painting cannot be a wholly worshipful experience for the artist making it. It is unlikely, however, that the viewer will have the same experience.

In the same way the Bible's characteristic metaphors can also become stale. Consider the stunned reaction of Nicodemus when Jesus coins the metaphor: "You must all be born again" (John 3.7). Nicodemus stutters his reply, "How can this be?" Two thousand years later the phrase "born again" will not surprise many people in the same way. It has been used so often.

So, from the Bible's example the visual artist can quickly grasp the importance of new metaphor in conveying religious ideas. Our belief places great emphasis on abstract words like faith, forgiveness, joy, and love. These are not concepts which are easy to depict. As a result the artist looks for new images which will give glimpses of the idea they wish to treat. The image of a mountaineer held by a single rope may be used to illustrate faith, or that of waves on the beach to treat the theme of forgiveness.

The artist aims to coin new metaphors, and make new combinations that cause us to puzzle and make the necessary effort to understand. The world can be seen as a diverse store of objects, ideas, and environments, and this book encourages you to play with them for the (sometimes) serious purpose of exploring and communicating what you find as you explore the Bible. Which leads us to the third question:

How can the artist explore the Bible itself?

There are some things about Bible study which remain the same whether you are setting out to draw a picture, or whether you are mulling over tomorrow's sermon. These basic rules cannot be forgotten.

1. Aim to read passages in context.

2. Seek God's guidance to help you understand a passage.

3. Look for the general principles taught in the passage before you leap in to ask what it might mean to you today.

4. Above all approach the text with humility, believing that in it we come face to face with God.

The arts are not a special tool which will help you get to grips with everything in the Bible. In fact it is really the other way round — a knowledge and practical trust in the Bible will help you see the world the right side up with the result that your art — or indeed any activity — will be enriched.

On the other hand there are some approaches to Bible study which can particularly help the visual artist. We've already seen how, if people are to be creative, they must not feel threatened and must be willing to experiment. The same can be said for creative Bible study.

It's important not to be threatened by things you don't immediately understand. Instead approach such "problems" positively. If you can't understand a passage, or have a question, don't just forget it or skip over it. Most Bibles have a few blank pages at the back and here is a perfect use for them. Every time you encounter something that you can't quite grasp, make a note of it. Every time you discover an explanation which satisfies you, scratch the troublesome passage off the list. Not only will this help you understand the particular passages but it will also help you develop an honest, relaxed approach to Bible.

The guidelines below will hopefully further relax you, help free your imagination, and encourage you to take chances with the Bible.

Read through the guidelines as a whole to start with. They are gathered under four main headings but they are not steps you use one after another. In fact, in practice, the process of Bible study suggested here will probably go something like this: You read a passage. You concentrate on one of the approaches suggested below. You make a few notes.

Your notes suggest to you some connection with other passages. In looking these up you make a few more notes, which in turn connect with . . . and so on, until your notebook begins to look like an aerial view of a motorway interchange. There will be side roads which seem at the time to be distractions, but which later you will realize led to the main event.

In fact you will quickly realize that running through most of the guidelines are two related methods: lists, and combining ideas. First, the value of making lists. You will make your own lists in the early stages of most design projects. Such lists will contain anything that comes to mind when you think of the project or passage you are dealing with. Most of these items will not be used in the finished concept or design but the list making process can speed you to a solution.

The second common factor in these guidelines is the importance of making connections between ideas, characters, and themes that run through the Bible. Experiment with these approaches until you discover what makes your Bible study exciting and informative. It will take some time, but then everything worthwhile does.

1. Imagine you were there

Much of the Bible is story — recounting God's dealings with his people in the real world. So imagine you were there, and try to picture the scene. Try to read between the lines and fill in the details you are not told about. Exodus 5.1–21, for example — what was it like as Moses walked into the Pharoah's palace to deliver an ultimatum? Moses, who complained to God that he wasn't very good at public speaking?

As you read the passage, jot down the answers to a few questions like: Who else was there? How were they dressed? What were they feeling? What did they say? How did Moses feel? Draw a sketch-plan of Pharoah's room as Moses saw it.

This effort to read between the lines — and fill in the unspoken detail — is worthwhile because it immediately sets free your imagination. While your imagining might not be historically correct it will help you grasp the feel of a story.

It also helps you to look at events from new perspectives. What would a guest at the wedding at Cana have said about Jesus' miracle of turning water into wine (John 2.1–11)? What would the "wine-waiter" say?

2. Note the way a passage is written and how it communicates

The Bible is not just "story". It contains poems, love songs, proverbs, laws, and much more besides. Each style of writing has its own characteristics.

In the Old Testament, for example, the Psalms are written in the then current form of Hebrew poetry. An idea is stated:

"Happy are those who reject the advice of evil men . . ."

and then the next line repeats the same idea in different words

" . . . who do not follow the example of sinners" (Psalm 1.1).

In the New Testament we find that Jesus often speaks in parables, Paul often speaks in complex arguments. Mark's style is terse and strong, Luke's more systematic and organized.

Try to build a list which records all the types of communication that you find in the Bible. Begin with the likely — Isaiah's prophecies, Paul's letters — then add the more obscure — Moses' censuses, Luke's genealogy, Samson's riddles.

Note alongside each item the particular *features* of that style. Is it formal like an official record, or informal like a family story?

Note *why* you think that style is used. Is it best at getting across facts, opinions, or feelings?

Note *other passages* where that style is used.

This list will become useful in two ways. It will open your mind to the many ways in which God does communicate — and possibly suggest to you some new or unlikely visual approaches. If you've been particularly gripped by Luke's genealogy could you, for example, make use of a family tree in your forthcoming church publicity?

Your list will highlight the fact that the Bible chooses a style of communication suitable to its original audience — a principle that applies as much to the visual arts as any communication. As Jesus used events and objects that his audience knew well in order to make his parables memorable, so we must take into account the knowledge and experience of our audience in our communication.

3. Note the imagery used in the passage

On page 2 we looked at biblical use of metaphor and simile. Now is your chance to begin to record those images, to organize them into categories, and so to start concentrating on those images that particularly appeal to you as an artist.

Is it Psalm 31.3 which describes God as a fortress? Or Proverbs 8 which personifies wisdom as a beautiful woman?

Again, creating a list should help you. Later this list of images will stimulate your creative activity. Let's just look now at one particular example. What metaphors are used to describe Jesus? Your list might begin:

JESUS

- The lamb of God
- The redeemer
- The door
- The vine
- The bread of life

- Living water
- The way
- The word
- The light
- The servant etc

Alongside each image note places where this image is used, and other images to which it relates. For example, alongside "the vine", you might note the image of God as "the gardener", or Paul's teaching about Christians "bearing fruit". Note modern parallels as well.

In summary, this process will:

■ Help you record the most memorable biblical images

■ Help you see how images relate to one another

■ In the long run, lead you to create your own metaphors

4. Make connections

We've already seen the value of making connections between passages. We can take this further.

Relate what you are reading to the story-line of the Bible as a whole. For example, how does the coming of Jesus fulfil the hopes of the Psalmist expressed in Psalm 22? Or where do the stories of Abraham and Joshua fit in the overall Old Testament story of how God's people were chosen and led by God to their promised land?

Look also for other passages about the same character. A cross-reference Bible or concordance is a help. Having found other passages, what do they add to your knowledge of that person?

The different Gospels often report the same events. For instance, Jesus' baptism by John appears in Matthew 3.13–17, Mark 1.9–11, Luke 3.21–22, and John 1.29–34. Ask yourself how they differ. Reading them all will increase your awareness of the meaning of the event and the approach of each writer.

5. Explore Bible themes

This takes the process of "making connections" to its logical conclusion. As you read the Bible, look for the themes that run through it. This has the effect of linking together the otherwise unrelated stories and characters.

Any one passage will usually connect with a number of different Bible themes. Try to spot them for yourself. For example when Jesus heals a man with a paralysed hand (Mark 3.1–6) the story relates to themes such as:

■ Physical healing

■ Spiritual healing

■ Conflict with the Pharisees

■ The Sabbath

■ Law and freedom

Read the passage for yourself, and you can probably add others.

This pinching of the brain will help keep you alert, giving you a new perspective on over-familiar passages, and a quicker recognition of the significance of less familiar ones.

It can be helpful, therefore, to build up a general list of Bible themes. The list below is to set you thinking. It is a small part of what could be recorded. It gathers themes under general headings. Some of the themes will immediately suggest visual interpretation. Others are quite abstract and may be difficult to render into visual terms at all. But as no two people are alike, a theme which doesn't excite your neighbour may well motivate you, or vice versa.

You will also find that this list of themes soon begins to overlap with your list of images — see 3 above. Indeed the value of a general list is that Bible themes, images, ideas, subjects, and characters are almost always interrelated. You cannot look at the theme of water, for instance, without it triggering immediate connections. The theme of cleansing for instance, or the image of Jesus as the water of life — or Moses leading Israel across the Red Sea, or miraculously bringing water gushing from a rock.

A general list can suggest other ideas that may have a bearing on your subject.

■ **God the Father**

the merciful God	God's anger
the faithful God	God's plan
the forgiving God	God's promises
the power of God	the alpha and the omega
the wisdom of God	the judge
God's memory	ever present
God's provisions	tolerates no rivals

■ **Christ**

the lamb of God	the son of man
the annointed one	Immanuel — God with us
the redeemer	the way
prophet, priest, and king	the Son of David
the first-born	the word
the door	the day-star
the vine	the light
the bread of life	the servant
living water	

9

■ The Holy Spirit

breath
wind
fire
dove
filling Christians
gift-giver

■ Symbols associated with God's revelation

the rock
the fountain
manna
light
tree
tower
fire
mountain
foundation

■ Miracles

casting out spirits
feeding
healing
raising from the dead
extraordinary phenomena in the natural world
creating confusion among enemies

■ Human activities

labouring
planting and harvesting
building
making and shaping
resting or sleeping
eating and drinking
planning and scheming
marrying
teaching
stewardship
listening and hearing
remembering the past
making music
going to war
praying

■ Human attitudes

pride
love
deceit
jealousy
anger
fear
faith
conceit
care for others
hope
meekness
the "hardened" heart
wilful ignorance
rebelliousness

10

■ **The church and Christ's followers**

the dwelling place of God

the sanctuary

the church as a flock

the church as an olive tree

true worship

assembly of God

the church as a lampstand

Mt. Zion

household of God

family of God

the body of Christ

a city

■ **Types**

the wise king

the prudent man

the drunk

the beggar

the weak or infirm

the rebel

the fool

the wise woman

the righteous man

the neighbour

the friend

the heathen

the hypocrite

the idol

the servant

the master

the soldier

the athlete

husband and wife

father and son

■ **The cause of the poor**

exiles and captives

strangers

restoration

respect for the land

■ **Images**

resurrection and rebirth

eternal life

true worship

the spirit

the flesh

We have left blank pages at the back of the book to allow you to add other ideas. The important thing, however, is not the list itself but the ability, which lists can assist, to see the themes which run through the Bible.

Illustration and fine art

The word "illustration" in the arts refers to a visualizing activity which takes its lead from a verbal source. So, for instance, the pictures in Bibles are illustrations derived from the stories in the text.

The fine arts, for those who value the distinction, are a more personal expression which do not need to be immediately clear. Some painters and theorists feel that illustration is therefore less important than "pure art", in that illustration must always serve the thing it illustrates.

I believe the Bible provides scope and inspiration for both illustration and fine art. Human life is the ultimate theme of the artist, and the Bible, needless to say, is full of "life". It reveals the frightening truth about us. This is a rich source for the painter to explore. However, in many contexts where clear explanation is the aim, then ideas, events, or principles in specific Bible passages are of utmost importance. Thus an illustration is most appropriate.

Illustration does not always have to emulate the look of things, though. A good illustration can be a symbol of the thing, a parallel, or contrast. The essential ingredient is the pointer which directs attention to the heart of the matter.

See for yourself the various effects that can be achieved by types of illustration by looking at the examples opposite. Which illustration, would you say, was best: for children, for people learning to read, for you, for your church?

Conclusion

For the Christian, the purpose of the arts is to return God's gifts to him — with interest. We are to develop the raw material God gives us. The trouble is that God has been so extravagant in his giving. There are too many gifts to develop. We haven't time to do justice to them all.

A combination of Bible exploration and creative experimentation

He will . . . go and look for the lost sheep (Matthew 18.12)

can begin to wake us up. Jesus invites the little children to come to him. Children who want to play. Children with silly questions. Children who want a story, or want to be shown something new. Little children with an insatiable appetite to learn and share what they have learned. The play of the arts, under the benevolent gaze of our all-creating Lord can help us recover a joy and excitement in his world. We will want more from the source of our gifts. We will want to praise, to cry out against all that destroys, and continually be amazed by the nature and character of our God.

2. "But I can't draw!"

This chapter is for anyone who can hold a pencil. It is not a textbook on drawing, and doesn't have twelve steps to dynamic portraits. Instead it contains a number of drawing games, some of which are rather bizzare. The games are a kind of warm-up for what follows, for you will soon discover that even if you "can't draw", your scribbles and scrawls are still important tools for exploration and expression. The games should provide quite a lot of enjoyment; they may tempt you to draw in your spare time. They can be used in lots of ways, on your own or with a group. But before introducing the games, it is worth considering the nature of drawing itself.

Everyone has drawn something. You probably did so today. It may have been a doodle while on the phone, or a map to show where you live. Perhaps it was a more "serious" drawing of something you wished to remember or tried to visualize. Of course, if we really need to recall things we can press the button on our auto-focus, auto-wind, auto-exposure, waterproof, auto-processing, camera. But technical wizardry doesn't always satisfy the need. There are still tasks for which the humble pencil is unsurpassed.

For drawing is not automatic, and therein lies its strength. Drawing records a chain of thoughts and decisions, and doing it blows dust off the mind. Some people seem to think better with a pencil in their hand. It just wouldn't be the same with a camera.

The pencil and the camera

When photography was invented, it had a mixed reception. Some artists hailed it as "Rembrandt perfected" or as "the pencil of nature". The English painter Landseer dubbed it "foe-to-graphic-art". The source of the furore, naturally, was the fact that the camera could do in a moment what painters had trained a life-time to perform. Or at least, so it appeared. The camera could make a faithful likeness, and in the nineteenth century likenesses were highly prized.

Curiously, the tension between photography and the arts has not entirely relaxed over the years. We still regard photographs as authoritative, even though we can look at a photo of a loved one and say "oh, no, that's not him at all!". Photos are our prime means of exchanging visual information, so there is a sense in which all visual images are measured against the standard of the photo.

Drawing is different. When someone sits down to do a drawing, it is a commitment. First, because the process takes time, second, because to draw is to concentrate, and third, because drawing is an attempt to understand the thing being drawn. The impersonality of the camera is not possible with the pencil.

For someone who hasn't drawn since childhood, the first experiments with a still-life or portrait are exasperating. The pencil goes adrift, shapes take on strange proportions and seem to mock the effort. It is very hard work indeed. Yet with practice, drawing becomes easier; even relaxing. The person who draws will notice more, take in subtle changes in facial expression, see how the light falls through the curtains, and how a child sprawls on the floor. These things as such may not seem important, but when considered by a sensitive artist they can become highly significant. It should also be true that the person who cares to draw the world will also care about the world they draw. They will be more alert and alive to their surroundings. In our rather narcissistic age that can't be a bad thing.

What is a good drawing?

Children will answer this question quickly: a good drawing is one that looks just like the real thing. They don't start out thinking this way, but they soon acquire this standard opinion. Precise renderings are almost like magic, and we marvel at the artist who can not only draw accurately, but quickly. When people say that they can't draw, they usually mean that they haven't learned how to copy.

This equation of drawing with rendering is most unfortunate. After all, the camera does its job very well — why should we try to compete with it? In point of fact, anyone can learn to draw accurately. The accuracy of a drawing is a matter of coordination between the eye and the hand. Given enough time and practice, anyone who can hold a pencil can learn to draw a good likeness. This can be seen from the educational programmes of nineteenth-century schools where everyone (but particularly girls) underwent strenuous training in drawing "well". Sure enough, they all learned to draw "accurately". What these academic drawings lack is any sense of fun or excitement.

They are clinical demonstrations of ability, done to satisfy the requirements of a "proper" education.

Drawing has much more to offer. Though there is no doubt that ability to draw accurately is a great asset to the artist, there is a more crucial element. That is the ability to find something which leaps into the imagination. Something that makes the artist want to draw. It can be a quality of the object, a sense of the environment, or even marks on the page of the drawing itself. It is a metaphor waiting to be made. This desire to tell is the essence of art. Drawing should say "Look at this!" or "What do you feel?" They needn't shout it, of course. Truthful, perceptive vision, coupled with technical proficiency and imagination will probably produce a good drawing. But without zeal, some love of the thing, and an urge to tell, that drawing will be tepid.

Aspects of drawing

As you spend time with pencil and paper, also think about the actual process of drawing. Attempts to understand the "mechanics" of the process can improve the result.

Drawing relies on looking. This is true even for blind artists. Either you look at something in your surroundings, or you "look" at something in your mind. For most of us, the images in our mind are rather vague faded imprints for the world outside. The mental images are not just snapshots, though. What image do you have of a hippo, for example? You have probably seen hundreds of photos, and half a dozen real creatures. The result? A picture in your mind which is not taken from any particular angle, which may or may not be in colour, and which is probably wholly inadequate for you to use in drawing a hippo. Yet the mental picture seems to be "clear".

How about looking at the world outside? We don't really notice very much there, either. We unconsciously "filter out" most of what is in front of us. The looking required in drawing is very complex, for we look at the "thing", at our mental file-box, and at the marks on the paper. Every new mark forces us to again scan the reference and see if the mark is "right". We look at the object and the mark we have just made, because both will influence our next mark. Drawing is a dynamic process of communication.

There is a house over there. To me it is an ordinary, turn-of-the-century brick semi. The builder who sees it sees that the bricks are cracking and that the gutters leak. To the postman it is number 94, taking nine monthly magazines; to the neighbour across the street it is dear old Mrs. Fiblock's place. Each viewer will see the same house, but will understand it differently — they will see what they know. The mind directs the eyes, and the eyes direct the mind.

This paradox is at the heart of the drawing activity — and is the source for much of the excitement in the process. The mind can juggle appearances, find parallels, make contrasts or create new metaphors. A drawing emerges.

The finished drawing then becomes an "object", and subject to the same interpretative process when people look at it. Its meaning can change. The response of the maker will never be the same as the response of the casual viewer.

These complicated thought and feeling processes lie below the surface when you are drawing. It is a good thing, for otherwise the pencil could hardly do more than twitch. By drawing, all categories of perception are enriched, not least the mental library. The image of the hippo becomes sharper, the hand moves more quickly to record a remembered characteristic, similarities between things come to mind . . .

Technical tips... Drawing

A few bits of advice for drawing:

■ Use a fairly soft pencil (3b or 4b) for a good black mark. Don't always sharpen it to a syringe-like point, but experiment with ways of getting different qualities of line. Generally, a blunt pencil is better than a sharp one as it is easier to make transitions from line to tone.

■ Try not to get in the habit of making twenty inconclusive lines rather than one positively wrong one. Try to minimize the total number of strokes. If you see that a line isn't right, consider drawing another single line on top, rather than fidgetting. The goal is an economy of marks.

■ Before you start to draw, look at the subject (if you are drawing from life) and try to imagine how it will fall on the paper. Visually compare sizes of things . . . the distance from the top of the basket to the table is about the same as the distance from the side of the apple to the book, etc. This can help avoid gross distortions of proportion.

■ Look at the shapes formed by the space between objects, as well as at the objects themselves. This so-called "negative space" can be a great help in establishing proportions and a sense of depth.

■ Try drawing with other tools — a bamboo stick, a brush, a bit of cardboard, a string dipped in ink — I'm serious! This will broaden your ideas about the kind of marks which are possible. The less controllable tools can sometimes produce beautiful results.

■ If you make a "bad" drawing, don't throw it away. Look at it a month later and be encouraged.

■ A few fast sketches at the beginning of a period of drawing can help to loosen your hand. Try not to hold the drawing tool too tightly.

■ Drawing regularly for a short time is better than drawing infrequently for a long time.

The drawing games

As you play the following drawing games, remember that although the skills of depiction are a great asset, they aren't the only part of drawing. Many famous artists can't depict very well. Some "cheat" and project photos onto a canvas and trace them. The end result can still be excellent. So don't worry if your lines don't meet up or if a portrait looks like a month-old grapefruit. Press on. The games will help you skirt some of the problems of not being technically proficient.

The first six you can play on your own, or with others. The last three require a group.

They are not games in the competitive sense. There are no "winners" or "losers". Some drawings will be better than others, and some people will do particularly well at some games. All these games involve play, wit, and strategy.

If you intend to use these games in a group the best group size is six to ten, but the games have proved effective with groups of twenty and more. Next to each title is an indication of how long a group should take for the game. The games should generate a spirit of curiosity, high spirits, and an interest in the process of drawing itself.

The notes which follow the descriptions are intended to help you think about and discuss aspects of the creative process. Do with them as you wish.

All of these games have been tried on "non-artists". Many excellent drawings have resulted — not so much because they were "suitable for framing", but because they show the result of highly inventive thinking. Have fun!

1. Heads up! (15 minutes)

Look in a mirror, and draw your own face. Or, if you are in a group, sit in a circle and draw the face of the person opposite.

The catch is that you are not allowed to lift your pencil from the paper *or* look at the paper. It requires real force of will not to look down. Try to move your pencil in precise correlation with the movements of your eyes. This is impossible, of course, but try anyway.

The results will amuse everyone. The drawings will obviously be of faces, but you will marvel that you have really drawn eyes on stalks, or grins on top of ears.

The same technique can be applied to drawing anything. Some people who have enjoyed this game have practiced to the point of being able to make things "meet up".

To add sheer terror to this game, try it with your other hand.

Notes

■ By depriving participants of the normal means of checking the progress of a drawing, a great sensitivity to the feel of the pencil develops. One becomes aware of the path of the eye, too. The initial embarrassment of staring at one another's head is soon replaced by the weight of concentration. A sense of apprehension in this exercise is quite normal.

■ Drawings made by this method almost always have pleasing visual properties. They have aberrations of proportion and placement that would not occur even if we were to try to create a stylized face. The human face is the most significant of all the components of our visual environment. Why is a reshuffling of the elements of a face so intriguing?

HEADS UP!

DON'T LOOK AT THE
PAPER, AND DON'T
LIFT THE PENCIL.

2. Contour lines (20 minutes)

The object of this exercise is to experience the way in which space is broken up by the things in it. We are normally accustomed to looking at objects, not the empty space around them. Yet for the artist the space between objects is very important — if for no other reason than the fact that the "empty space" has to be drawn too!

Set up a simple still life: a bottle, a loaf of bread, basket of fruit, a tea-towel, or whatever. Start your drawing by making a horizontal line from the left edge of the paper. When the line reaches the place corresponding to the position of an object, make the line bend as if it were running along the surface of that object (see illustration). For example, if the line bumps into an orange it will curve upwards or downwards depending on where the line meets the edge. After much wiggling the line will reach the other side of the paper. Start a second line parallel to the first, at a distance of about a quarter of an inch, and continue in the same way until you have a whole field of lines. The effect should resemble the scene as viewed through a venetian blind.

Notes

■ The pattern of lines can be very pleasing, even if the result is not "accurate".

■ This is an excellent exercise for experiencing depth. The pencil has to feel its way along the surfaces as there is no usual "line around the edges".

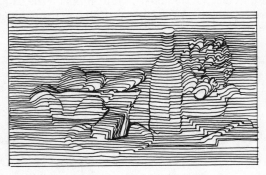

CONTOUR LINES

DRAWINGS MADE THIS WAY CAN LOOK
NICE WITH PALE WASHES OF COLOUR.

3. X-ray vision (40 minutes)

You have probably seen "cut away" drawings of motorcars, buildings, and machines. These are usually very precise and detailed. Try a looser version of this technique to draw the house where you live or where you are meeting. Draw the whole building as if it were semi-transparent and you were hovering above it. You'll need a rubber for this one. You'll also spend a fair bit of time walking around trying to see through walls.

Notes

■ This is a good way to help see how things fit together. We are accustomed to looking at surfaces. By the time you have finished your drawing you will have a new understanding of an environment which is extremely familiar but probably never "understood". You will have constructed an image which could not have been photographed.

■ At a philosophic level this exercise has many parallels in our thought processes. We see a situation, object, person, or environment, and at once start filling in details, or forming opinions based on surface observations. This exercise is also a pattern for Bible study. If we "dwell in God's house" shouldn't we also try to understand how the different parts of God's revelation interrelate? As we study the Bible we have the opportunity to do just that. We can read "from different angles" and deepen our grasp of the whole.

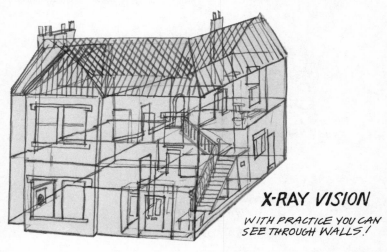

X-RAY VISION

WITH PRACTICE YOU CAN SEE THROUGH WALLS!

4. Eye-shift (10 minutes)

Try to do a drawing from an imaginary vantage point somewhere in the room. For instance, pretend that you are sitting on the opposite side of the room, or that your eye is in one corner of the ceiling, or floor.

Notes

■ This is excruciatingly difficult, but well worth the toil. What is it that we say about trying to see it from another perspective? One little moral from this game might be that we shouldn't be too glib about saying "I see" to someone else's comment!

■ The ability to place your viewpoint is important in picture composition. A low vantage point, for example, makes very dramatic compositions; a high one creates the feeling of space. The mind's eye can be trained to "see round" objects or where your picture involves a moving object, into one characteristic pose.

EYE - SHIFT
LOOK OVER YOUR OWN SHOULDER

5. Absent objects (5 minutes each)

A simple variation on the classic children's party game. Place an object on the table for about half-a-minute. Remove it, and then make a drawing.

Notes

■ This technique is also useful as a means to train the visual memory. If you have spent an hour-or-so making a sketch of, say, an outdoor scene, it can be firmly fixed in your mind if you try to do a second drawing from memory when you get home. Keep it up and your visual memory will require bigger filing cabinets.

6. Emotions (5 minutes each)

Try to draw a face showing one of the following emotions: anger, fear, elation, exhaustion, jealousy, love, etc. If you're in a group you can have fun watching everyone screwing up their faces trying to get the feel of something they can't see. This exercise will give a new appreciation of the skills of the cartoonist.

Notes

■ We can read expressions with great skill and speed. Why, then, is it so difficult to be at all precise in drawing them? How much of an expression depends on other factors, such as position of the body, and voice?

DISCOURAGEMENT

DETERMINATION

7. Object and environment (8 minutes per round)

This is one of the most popular drawing games. The person on your left gives you the name of an object and the one on your right an environment. Let's see . . . an octopus and a phone box . . . a bird bath and an igloo . . .

You must draw that object, in that environment, as best you can. There are many possible approaches, but the results of this game are almost always humorous. You may well wish to save the results.

Allow eight minutes per round, and play about four rounds.

OBJECT AND ENVIRONMENT
"A WATER FOUNTAIN AND A VOLCANO"

Notes

■ Why do people usually try to make their drawings into stories?

■ The random combination of unlikely things often can be used as a creative tool. Being confronted with "illogical" elements throws us in at the deep end and allows a freer play of thought.

■ A slightly more structured version of this game can be an asset in artistic problem-solving. If you make a list of every conceivable aspect of a topic and then try random combinations from the list, you often discover new ideas.

■ This game also stretches the visual memory. Isn't it hard to remember what things look like! The next time you see the object in question you will undoubtedly look more closely — just what shape is a giraffe's jaw?

8. Emotional shapes (12 minutes)

This game is the most "abstract" so far, in that there is nothing "specific" on which to focus. Try to make a drawing which expresses one of the following: power, speed, light, space, time, serenity, height, cold, security, etc. Inclusion of words in the drawing is not on. Don't tell anyone what theme you have chosen.

At the end of the game each drawing is numbered and held up for everyone to see. Each person writes down the word suggested by the drawing, until at last the artist tells what concept they were illustrating.

Notes

■ This is a difficult exercise, and a taste of the use of metaphor in the arts. None of the above themes can be depicted as they are. All must be approached through an image, experience, or environment which is common to others. If you had a terrible experience with eggs as a child, your idea of terror may be a hard-boiled egg. But you cannot blame someone for labelling your image "fragility".

■ Isn't it curious how often we transfer our own feelings onto the world around us? We talk about the "lonely moors" because we feel lonely there, or about "a refreshing dawn" because we feel refreshed. How much of our seeing is conditioned by the way we feel?

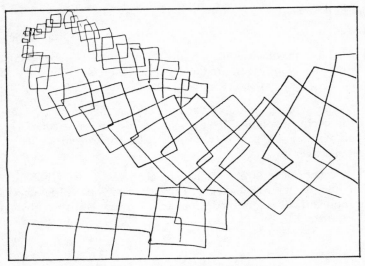

EMOTIONAL SHAPES GAME
A DRAWING OF "TIME"

GUESS WHAT EMOTIONAL SHAPE THIS IS SUPPOSED TO ILLUSTRATE?
(LIGHT)

9. The drawing game (10 minutes each)

All of the previous games are drawing games, but this is the one that many people are most eager to play. Others simply find it too exhausting. The idea is simple: you have ten minutes to draw whatever you are told to draw by the person on your left. An additional initial period of five minutes is granted for everyone to come up with assignments for each other. People quite naturally try to come up with the most difficult or ludicrous themes they can imagine . . . oil rigs doing the can-can, the dreams of a retired mushroom-farmer, a badger building boxcars . . .

The best solutions are invariably those which add yet another twist to the assignment — the oil rig is shown juggling oil barrels (the can-can) — well, it does get corny . . . Write the title on each drawing. You'll certainly want to save your best efforts.

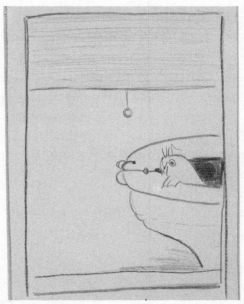

"A CATFISH SCALING THE EMPIRE STATE BUILDING"
TYPICAL GOOD SOLUTION TO A DRAWING
GAME PROBLEM - THE PARTICIPANT HAS
DRAWN JUST ENOUGH TO CONVEY THE IDEA.

27

Notes

■ This taxing game has three parts: coming up with the assignment, figuring a way to tackle it, and doing the drawing. The drawing itself isn't usually as difficult as trying to interpret the assignment — and stay within the time limit!

■ The giving of assignments and the ultimate showing of the results are the key to the success of this game as a social affair. The challenge of making it difficult for the other person and handling the problem you are given is very much like other games. But the activity is quite different from other games in the scope it gives for the imagination. After playing for a while you may want to hear from the others how they go about generating assignments or solving them. Are there any points that the best solutions have in common?

 The drawing games

Here are some suggestions as to how you can use these games:

■ On your own, to pass the time, or to develop your drawing skills
■ As part of an arts day or arts workshop (see page 115)
■ As ice-breakers or looseners in any group situation
■ As a prelude to any of the activities in this book
■ As an introduction to a discussion on the use of visual arts in the church
■ As party games

Don't try too many at a sitting. Two or three is ample.

Conclusion

If you have enjoyed these exercises, invent some of your own. If you can find a group of people who wish to meet regularly to draw, you can introduce the occasional drawing game to keep the evening moving. Informal drawing groups can be a great help in the development of artistic skills because they provide a social context for the drawing activity and allow "feedback". They also prepare people for working in a group. As we will see later, group efforts are often very important in using the arts in service of the church and community.

Drawing is a rewarding activity. It prompts inventive thinking and intensifies perception. It is undoubtedly hard work, but the sort of hard work which satisfies and stimulates. Above all, the effort to understand things which a drawing requires leads the eye and mind beyond the mere surface. In an age which is proud of the modern skills of making visual replicas and synthetic experience, drawing prevents us from becoming passive.

These features of the drawing process apply to other areas of our lives. As Christians we are called to be "salt" — preserving what is good and bringing out the flavour of the world. To do this we must struggle to remain alert. The Bible is full of things which jolt safe, insulated perception. If we study it and at the same time strive to see more clearly, we will be in a good position to explain the wonder of God's grace to others.

Drawing is a basic tool for expressing ideas. In much of what follows you will find that drawing enriches your study, and helps make your thinking more specific. It helps explain ideas to others and records the development of your reflections. Keep pencil and paper handy!

3. Images to explain or teach

Most churches have some meetings which are informal, and others which are rather more formal. In the formal service of worship the verbal symbols of preaching are usually central. Many speakers know, however, that they can significantly improve their presentation by using simple visual aids, or by enlisting the help of an "artist" to provide either drawings for an overhead projector, or artwork for a flipchart.

The aim of this chapter, then, is to introduce some simple ways of illustrating a talk with:

■ Props
■ Masks

then to explore, through a worked example, the techniques involved in:

■ Preparing a series of drawings to illustrate a talk
■ Presenting those drawings on a flipchart or an overhead projector

Visual and verbal

The Bible has many references to teaching. Some of the most memorable talk about visual reminders. For example, in Deuteronomy 11, God tells his people as they enter the promised land to make use of visual aids.

> [18] "Remember these commands and cherish them. Tie them on your arms and wear them on your foreheads as a reminder. [19] Teach them to your children. Talk about them when you are at home and when you are away, when you are resting, and when you are working. [20] Write them on the door-posts of your houses and on your gates. [21] Then you and your children will live a long time in the land that the LORD your God promised to give to your ancestors. You will live there as long as there is a sky above the earth . . ."

> (Deuteronomy 11.18–21)

No simple knot in the handkerchief here, but a memory-aid tied to wrists and forehead! God doesn't want his people to forget what he has said. And he knows how well-chosen images can help us to remember.

Have you ever asked the way and got lost before the explanation was finished?

"So, that was right under the bridge, down past the park and then left . . ."

"No, right past the park, then left . . ."

"Right, er, I mean yes . . . Right, then left . . . and then left again at the third set . . ."

"Fourth set of lights . . ."

"Oh yes, well thanks very much."

You are in a muddle, but it would be too embarrassing to have it all repeated. You set off, drive round the corner and look for someone else to ask.

How much easier it is with a map! There are some things which can hardly be explained without pictures.

But there are others that cannot be explained without words. Visual expressions have built-in constraints. Suppose you want to make a political cartoon to say that So-and-So is a tyrant. It wouldn't be difficult. There are any number of exaggerations possible in a drawing which would make So-and-So appear quite despicable. Give him beady eyes and a hawk nose for starters . . .

Now try to do the opposite, and make a cartoon to say that So-and-So is the finest statesman alive . . . see? How would you do it without making something which looked sentimental and silly? In this particular case it seems that the deck is stacked — cartoons work by means of exaggerations which are very suitable for making critical statements, or at least for recasting affairs in a humorous form. The medium is limited. Try precisely the same exercise with words and there is no obstacle.

But put pictures and words together and you have the most powerful means possible for conveying information, opinion, or ideas.

Visual and verbal languages are never equivalent. A picture created by good writing can never really be compared with a brilliant painting. The first leads us to form a mental equivalent for the words we read, while the painting presents visual information and moods that we may not be able to express in words. In this context, it is worth reflecting on the fact that God shows us something of his character in the natural world, but we only begin to truly understand him through Christ — the Word.

Sensitivity to the interaction between words and images will increase the scope of what can be communicated:

■ Words can be **titles or labels** for a picture, as in the familiar newspaper caption. As such, words provide a context which assist comprehension.

■ Words can present a **contrast** to the image, as can readily be seen in headlines for many adverts.

■ Words can cause an image to be understood in an unusual fashion, or at **several different levels**. For instance the words from the Ten Commandments, "Do not steal" could be accompanied by a picture of an employer's time clock. The words and image would thus point beyond themselves to an attitude of heart. The notion of stealing is removed from the usual associations of shoplifting, embezzling, or burglary.

THESE PLYWOOD LETTERS ARE ABOUT 8" HIGH AND ⅛ᵗʰ" THICK. THEY ARE CHANGED ACCORDING TO THE THEME OF THE SERVICE.

Simple visual aids

There are obviously some limitations to the sorts of images and visual aids which you might choose for a church meeting. One sunday-school teacher illustrated the story of Elijah and the prophets of Baal on Mount Carmel (1 Kings 18) by a rather dramatic device. He poured twelve cups of water on a model altar made from stones as he told the story. Unknown to the children, each cup of water had a thin layer of petrol on the top. At the crucial moment when Elijah prayed, the teacher struck a lighter behind the altar and out of sight of the children. Whump! Fire from heaven. Suffice it to say that the children were wide-eyed. But the demonstration overwhelmed the point it was trying to illustrate, and gave everyone a few anxious moments!

This case serves to illustrate some very important points about visual aids:

■ Don't lose sight of the story or principle you are illustrating.

■ Think about such obvious factors as safety and the length of time your contribution will take. An illustration which drags on isn't a good illustration. Try to be concise, clear and powerful.

■ Remember that images which look good on the table in front of you may not have the same strength when seen from the back of the church hall.

■ Try an idea out on friends first, before polishing up something no one but you will understand.

Though it is easy to agree these things and say, "Of course!", it is surprising how soon we can be carried away by enthusiasm, and forget basic rules of communication.

For a sermon illustration or talk, try to develop methods and styles which can be quickly executed and still appear fresh and interesting. Directness is the key. It is better to spend at least half of what little time you have in finding an appropriate image or concept. That's an important element in the success of the two ideas that follow, using simple props and masks.

 **Props**

An hilarious sketch for children (and adults) built around a few simple props. The theme is taken from Psalm 139 — how God orders his creation.

The props are a good quality adhesive-backed rubber nose, a rubber ear, two stick-on eyes, and half a table-tennis ball painted to resemble an eye-ball. These joke-shop ingredients are used to reflect on the fact that God created every part of us in a "wonderful" way. Read it for yourself:

> [13]You created every part of me;
>   you put me together in my mother's
>   womb.
> [14]I praise you because you are to be
>   feared;
>   all you do is strange and wonderful.
>   I know it with all my heart.
> [15]When my bones were being formed,
>   carefully put together in my mother's
>   womb,
>   when I was growing there in secret,
>   you knew that I was there—
> [16] you saw me before I was born.
> The days allotted to me
>   had all been recorded in your book,
>   before any of them ever began.
> [17]O God, how difficult I find your
>   thoughts;
>   how many of them there are!
> [18]If I counted them, they would be more
>   than the grains of sand.
>   When I awake, I am still with you.

(Psalm 139.13–18)

The patter can be something like this:

"Imagine what it would be like if your nose was on upside down? (Put on aforementioned nose.) It would fill up with rain, and when you sneezed you'd blow your hat off . . . Or what if you had an eye on the end of your finger? (Put the half-table-tennis ball on your finger.) Super-handy for finding bits of Lego under the sofa, and you could see around corners, and see if your keys were in your pocket . . . Ouch! a key in the eye . . ." etc.

You'll not find it difficult to lead to a serious conclusion.

Try it out... Masks

Simple masks can be very effective helps in telling a story. They needn't be worn. All you need to do is to mount faces on sticks (as in the illustration below) and paint them to represent the key figures in a story.

Each time a character speaks, the relevant mask is held up. Absolutely rudimentary, but kids love it.

Below are illustrations of masks you can use to tell the story of the Good Samaritan (Luke 10.25–37). With a few bold strokes the masks express the range of human emotions from fear to relief, pride to humility.

ROBBER

VICTIM

LEVITE

SAMARITAN

Drawings to illustrate a story

Often you will want to create a series of drawings to illustrate a story or talk.

There are some publications around which will cut a few corners for you. For example, selected illustrations from the *Good News Bible* are being made available on OHP acetates ready for you to use — there are some details on page 123.

But let's assume you want to start from scratch and create your own presentation. And let's assume, as well, that you aren't the speaker who'll be using these drawings. Someone else will be displaying your drawings at the appropriate moment — hopefully the right way up! It follows that your illustrations will have to be clear — because you won't be there to point out the bits of the drawing that others seem to be missing!

How would you proceed?

> ## Worked example... Illustrating a story

You've been asked to provide a set of overhead projector acetates to illustrate the parable of the Lost Coin (Luke 15.8–10). You know the illustrations will be used as part of a normal service in your church — not as a children's address. What's more this is a "first". Never before has such an approach been used in your normal services. Some responsibility . . . so take it seriously.

You should work through the following steps:

1. Explore the story or passage

The Lost Coin

8"Or suppose a woman who has ten silver coins loses one of them — what does she do? She lights a lamp, sweeps her house, and looks carefully everywhere until she finds it. 9When she finds it, she calls her friends and neighbours together, and says to them, 'I am so happy I found the coin I lost. Let us celebrate!' 10In the same way, I tell you, the angels of God rejoice over one sinner who repents".

(Luke 15.8–10)

The story is about finding the lost. The energy that the woman puts into searching for the coin is clear indication that for her the loss of the coin is no trifling matter. She lights a lamp and starts sweeping the house. When she finds it she has a celebration party.

On first reading you will probably have formed a mental picture of the scene, and this may be a good basis for making drawings. But before you set to work, look at the passage again. Ask yourself the all important question — **What is the purpose of the parable?** Jesus answers that when he says, "In the same way, I tell you, the angels of God rejoice over one sinner who repents."

Now the parable is both clearer and more complex. The lost coin belongs with the other coins, as part of the woman's possession. The thrust of the parable is the joy that rewards her energetic search. So God actively, patiently, searches for sinners. This picture is quite different from the popular image of people searching for a hidden, apathetic God! And when a sinner is restored, the angels rejoice. It is a shock to think that all of heaven is waiting for the long search to turn us up.

2. Consider possible visual approaches

There are now many more choices of visual interpretation. You could focus on the theme of "lost and found". Or on the popular misconception that God is aloof, or disinterested.

After working through some of the possibilities you may want to ring up the speaker and discuss them. As this is his first venture into the visual arts you may find it difficult to sell your idea:

"Hello John, listen, you know those OHP slides you want for the parable of the lost coin, well I have an idea . . . I mean, people don't think that a coin is worth much these days . . . and I thought that it would be better if we could sort of bring it up to date a bit . . .

"Yes . . . what do you have in mind?"

"Well, I was thinking . . . what do people today value in the same way? So I have done some sketches for the parable of the lost wallet . . . The scene opens with a woman digging down the crack of a car seat . . ."

"Mmm. Yes. Well, Roy, I'm not sure on this one. Perhaps we had better stick to the text. I see what you mean, but . . ."

Then again, he may say "Great", and you can get to work.

If you had been illustrating your own talk, of course, the problem of selling your ideas would vanish.

3. Make a storyboard

This is a simple series of empty rectangles of the right format for your final illustrations. These scaled down frames let you sketch out the sequence of images to see how they will tell the story. You write under each box the key action or title of the scene.

Now the Lost Coin is a very terse parable, and the whole story is really only five scenes: 1) the woman has ten silver coins; 2) she loses one; 3) she searches; 4) finds it; and 5) calls the neighbours to celebrate. If you wished to emphasize the idea that God searches for us, you could develop scene 3 into a number of slides to show where she searches, and how long she searches for. If you wished to emphasize celebration then you could develop scene 5.

After thinking this through, you decide to go for simplicity. As the parable will be told quite quickly, your drawings will be seen only briefly. There isn't much point in making highly detailed pictures. You can now concentrate on finding a suitable means of portrayal. Opposite is a suggestion for the slides. You will notice straightaway that there are eight slides, not five. The first is a title. This gives added drama as viewers wait to see what is coming. The last two slides reinforce the lesson of the parable. The seventh "zooms in" on the found coin to reveal a picture of a man, thus stressing the connection between the found coin and the repenting "sinner"; and the last slide is the words of Jesus' comment, framed by blaring trumpets.

In this case the story from the original parable has remained. In your proposed rewrite it would have changed. The point is not whether one approach is absolutely better than the other. Either could be effective. These are not the only possible interpretations, either. Two other parables in Luke 15 treat the same theme in different ways.

Technical tips... **Making overhead projector slides**

The actual preparation of overhead projector slides takes some care — note that:

■ The reason that the slides are more awkward than a normal drawing is that the base material is a sheet of plastic film. Many ordinary drawing materials will not work well on plastic film.

Storyboard illustrating the parable of the Lost Coin (Luke 15.8–10).

■ There are photographic means of turning drawings into overhead projector slides, but the process is costly.

■ It is possible to make slides from drawings using a plain-paper copier. If you use this technique be sure that you use a plastic film **which does not melt**. Diacetate or triacetate are best. Triacetate will also accept most conventional drawing materials. Both materials are available from graphic arts suppliers. Photocopiers fix the image on the surface by means of heat, and the wrong sort of film will turn to treacle on the drum. With the correct film, the copier is a very good way of transferring an image, though obviously it will only print black lines.

■ Special markers made for overhead slides are generally available. Because the film is transparent, tracing images from your drawings or from photographic reference is simple. When using markers it is best to check the drawing against a window so that it is possible to see what it will look like when projected. Images always look more intense on the film than when projected.

■ A heat-resistant colour film can be used to fill in large areas of solid colour, but again this is an expensive material. Surprisingly good results can be obtained by using coloured tissue-paper. This can be fixed to the acetate sheet by spraying it lightly with aerosol adhesive. Handle finished slides carefully, as they are easily scratched.

■ If possible, try the slides out before the final show. To avoid embarrassing fumbling with the slides, thin strips of card can be stuck to the edges of the projector to register each slide as it is slid into place. This will keep everything square and enable you to change slides very quickly.

■ Position the projector as high as possible to prevent distortion of the image.

■ Overlays are another useful device in teaching. For example, a basic map may be used with arrows, symbols, or images on overlays. With this method you could effectively trace the wanderings of the Israelites in the wilderness, or Paul's missionary journeys.

■ Other effects can be developed by making flat silhouette puppets. These are placed on top of a background slide, and can be manipulated by attaching thin sticks to the parts you want to move.

Back to the parable, however. What if your illustrations were not to be displayed on an overhead projector, but instead were going to be worked up into finished drawings on a flip chart, or on large pieces of card? How would that change things?

Well, very little to start with. You would still explore the passage, consider visual approaches, and make a storyboard. Your storyboard might need to change, of course, to accommodate the differences in media. For example the initial title slide might be less effective when drawn on a flip chart, so you might well change that one.

How do you now work up your basic sketches into artwork which can be appreciated by a large church congregation?

■ If you make an image to be held up in front of more than twenty people you will need bold, clear forms. Pencil, watercolour, and other delicate media tend to disappear at more than ten feet. Poster paint, large felt-tipped markers, collage with coloured papers, and chalks or crayons can give the image the necessary impact. Generally speaking, you can afford to miss out fine details. For example the bristles on the woman's broom really aren't that important — the overall impression is. Err on the side of making images which are too strong.

■ A twenty-by-thirty inch poster is the minimum size required for showing to groups of twenty-five or more. As large sheets of paper are difficult to handle, it is a good idea to tack a sheet of paper to a sheet of cardboard the same size. This is much cheaper than preparing artwork directly on to mounting board or illustration board.

■ Prepare sketches on paper before launching into a twenty-by -thirty inch poster. These sketches can be enlarged in many ways — some of which are explained in the next set of technical tips.

■ If you are very brave, it is possible to do a drawing while you, or someone else is telling a story. So called "chalk talks" are not too common any more, but they still hold a crowd. The trick is to carefully draw fine pencil lines on the paper indicating all of the forms of your drawing. No one will be able to see them except you and the smart-alec kid in the front row who shouts out that you are "cheating".

Working on a mid-tone paper (grey is probably best) lets you use white to good effect as well as the other colours. Bold strokes are better than "fussy" ones.

■ Have a good look at the environment in which the image will be displayed. Try to see how the light falls, what is in the background, how far the image will be from the back row, etc. These conditions should be in your mind as you set to work. For instance, if there are windows at the front of the hall, the speaker standing at the front might appear to the audience almost as a silhouette. A drawing would have to be very bold indeed to be seen.

■ Use the whole page! Think of the paper as a window through which the scene is observed. The area around the image is important, too.

Technical tips... Making enlargements

The scribble in your sketchbook looks wonderful, and you imagine how effective it will be as a big poster. But when you start redrawing it up to scale, it doesn't look the same, no matter how often you rub out and redraw. The paper soon begins to look like an old carpet underlay. You start on a fresh sheet . . .

This frustrating experience can be tempered if you bear the finished size of the drawing in mind while you are making sketches. A thin pencil line may have qualities which are difficult to repeat with a chunky black marker. Although practice will help you to anticipate some of the effects of changing scales, you will long for a simple way of enlarging your sketches. Try some of these:

■ Many photocopiers now have enlargement and reduction facilities. By repeated enlargement, very big images can be made. Due to the loss in quality from repeated enlargements you will probably have to touch up the final print, or trace it off.

■ If your original drawing is on graph paper, it is possible to copy it quite well by drawing a light grid to scale on your large sheet and noting where lines intersect the grid. This takes time and some accuracy.

■ If you can, get hold of an epidiascope or opaque projector, to "project" your original outline onto a larger sheet, which you can then trace. Alternatively it is possible to project a drawing made on ordinary paper by using an overhead projector. Draw with heavy lines on thin paper, and then grease the paper. This makes the paper translucent enough for your lines to show up when projected. Messy, but it works.

■ For a very precise enlargement such as that required to enlarge lettering, you can use slides. A normal black and white negative of your drawing can be mounted in a slide-frame and projected. This should be clear enough to trace in all but the brightest rooms. This is particularly useful for drawing large maps, or for making drawings from photographs. Transfer lettering (such as Letraset) applied to clear plastic film will also give a crisp image when projected.

If possible, get someone to help you with this side of production.

Try it out... **Visual aids**

If you have been asked to create visual aids then it is likely that you will already have been given a passage or theme to present.

If not, then you can still sharpen your skills by working up a storyboard to illustrate a parable such as the Rich Man (Luke 19.18–30) for a specified event — for example a family service.

Better still, give some time to considering other possible uses for visual aids. For example:

■ Talks by missionaries or other Christian workers. How may talks have you heard which were illustrated by faded slides? You probably can't nip off to Ethiopia to make better ones, but you can help by making maps, charts, diagrams, or title slides.

■ House groups. If someone takes the time to prepare a chart of the kings of Judah for a study of 2 Chronicles, the historical context of the passage will be clearer. There are many things in the Bible which we read without seeing the overall context. Books like *The Good News Colour Reference Bible* (Bible Society, 1979), *The Illustrated Bible Dictionary* (IVP, 1980), or *The Lion Handbook to the Bible*, second edition (Lion, 1983), can provide you with first rate sources of such background material from which to make visual aids.

You will quickly think of others I'm sure — and in the process probably your mind will turn to how the artist cannot only help speakers and teachers in the church, but can offer a much wider ministry. The next chapter explores this potential further.

4. Images to inspire

In the last chapter we assumed your images were used as part of a talk. More often they must stand on their own, so this chapter looks at some wider uses of visual images in the life of the church, including:

- **A 35mm slide show**
- **Banners to decorate the church**
- **Backdrops**
- **Group murals**

Some of the activities in this chapter can be better done by a keen group than by one person, however talented. Working together with others is part of the thrill of the visual arts, and it is certainly a help in getting to grips with some of the deeper, more elusive themes of the Bible.

A 35mm slide show

If you are a keen photographer it is likely that you already have shoe-boxes full of old photos. If you organize this material and try to put it in some order, you may be surprised to find that you have the makings of a slide show. (If the photos are all of your t mily obscuring various national monuments, you would be very surprised indeed.)

If you normally shoot colour negative film, it might be the time to switch to slides. The 35mm slide is a very effective medium. In addition to stirring shots of the natural world, if you have a camera with a close-up lens (one which permits focusing to a distance of about twelve inches) it is possible to photograph drawings, collages, photographs, or small objects for use in a slide show. All of which makes the slide show a fascinating and versatile project.

Worked example... **A 35mm slide show**

Imagine that it is Easter and you have been asked to prepare a visual programme to help church members and visitors reflect on the meaning of Jesus' death and resurrection. The topic is "sacrifice". You have about five minutes to fill.

Even such a short show will take time and careful planning. You need to work out the images, possibly make props, take photos, edit, and organize a sound-track. What follows is an ambitious treatment.

1. Planning

First, estimate the number of slides you are likely to need. If the average time that a slide is on the screen is six seconds, you will need ten slides a minute, or fifty-plus slides. (Many commercial shows would figure on two seconds a slide!) At this stage you might try to get some money from the church *and* enlist the support of a photographer. A project like this can be handled by one person, but not without considerable time and energy. Materials won't be cheap either.

It is possible to make some slides without a camera, and other slides could be ordinary black and white (more later on this technique). So, assume that you will be able to get all of the colour work on one roll of thirty-six exposure film.

2. Exploring the theme

Having roughly established the technical requirements you can uncomfortably start work on the theme. Uncomfortably, because the first stage of such a project is daunting. The rows of empty frames on your storyboard are as vacant as your knowledge of the future. Where to start? You reach for the concordance. . . Soon you have the beginnings of a list of all the occasions in the Bible which mention sacrifice:

■ Cain and Abel

■ Abraham on the mountain with his son Isaac

(Before reading on, note down quickly any other instances that come to mind.)

Compiling the list will have stimulated your imagination and suggested some strong visual images. However, your show would not be very cohesive if you simply showed an image for each incident on your list. Read through the many texts and try to extract a few essential elements. Ask such questions as:

■ What is a sacrifice?

- Why is sacrifice performed?
- Why does God demand sacrifice?
- What rules does he set for the practice of sacrifice?
- What kind of sacrifice does God hate?
- What symbolism is attached to sacrifice?

This is a step closer. Now you have begun to examine not only the record of sacrifices in the Bible but the connection between them. As you continue your study, some things will strike you with such force that you will want to share them in the show. The concepts which we discover first-hand are the concepts we best communicate. For instance, it occurs to me as I read that all of life is sustained by sacrifice. In order for life to continue, another life must be given up; from micro-organisms to man. Against this background Christ's death makes sense. And no wonder Christ refers to himself as food and drink.

This idea suggests another link: sacrifice and food. Seen from this perspective (and it is not the only one), the texts open up. The sacrificial offerings of the Old Testament were carefully selected food. Only the best would do. In contrast to food offered to idols, the sacrifice is not to feed God, for he needs nothing. Instead it is a symbol, because the food fuels the fire that otherwise would consume the sinner. The value of the food placed on the altar is relinquished for the greater value of God's blessing.

The theme is rich and complex, and now you are asking if every picture you make will require researching a sermon. The only answer is that the more you study and reflect, the more you will understand. The more you understand and are moved by what you have learned, the more content can infuse your work. This sort of study has a cumulative effect. The study of one passage or incident will suddenly tie in with another. You cannot possibly examine all of these associations, but the more links you find in the themes of the Bible, the more you will find to say. The theme of sacrifice appears throughout the Bible, so it is not surprising that study leads you deeper and deeper into reflection.

3. Summarizing what you have discovered

To break the reverie, you have a deadline. All of the reading, reflection, and complex metaphors somehow have to be brought to bear on the preparation of a five-minute visual piece. You won't be able to pack everything in, so this stage is one of organizing. Select the idea or image which has most struck you, and make this the theme of the show. In five minutes you can just about communicate one idea, and you want to be sure that you communicate it well.

Suppose you select the image of food, as mentioned above. What you have discovered could be summarized:

■ Food and water are the symbols of life itself

■ For one life to continue, another must be given up

■ God provided food and water for his people in the wilderness

■ God demanded that food be offered up to himself, and this food had to be of the best quality

■ Jesus said that he was the bread of life, and that out of him flowed "living water"

■ The Lord's supper is a sign of our sharing in Jesus' death, and our continual feeding on him

Don't worry about writing points in any particular order. Try to condense the list by combining points. Ultimately you should be able to summarize the point of your show in one line. Thus the six points listed above could be summarized as: "Man cannot live on bread alone, but needs every word that God speaks." (Deuteronomy 8.3 as quoted by Jesus in Matthew 4.4.)

The second stage expanded the scope of the study, and then the third stage compressed it. This, of course, is exactly the method suggested earlier as suitable for the artist — set free the imagination, then organize the results. As you can now see, it is really a means of assisting clear thinking.

4. A creative strategy

How can you now interpret the results of your study in visual form? That will depend on understanding your audience, and on your interests, abilities, and resources. Below is an outline of one possible interpretation — yours would be different. The key stage, curiously, has already been reached by crystallizing the theme into a main point.

You **title** the show "Life through death". A taped sound-track will help link elements together, and can help enormously in making sure that images are understood.

There are now three major factors to attend to:

■ The development of the idea — **the plot**

- The **visual images**
- The **sound-track**

The second two must always work to support the first. This sounds like the most obvious, simple rule there is. True, but also the most broken. For instance, if you have a rapid succession of powerful images on the screen, you can't have a rapid series of important statements on the tape at the same time. Eyes take precedence, and the message on the sound-track won't get an ear in.

Think also about the **pace** of the show. Will it start with a bang, then slow down, and build steadily to a climax? Or start slowly, build to one peak, and level off? Quick changes can generate a quick pace, but so can slow changes accompanied by a dramatic sound track. Think about films, books, plays, or music that you like, and try to become sensitive to the way in which these forms develop their dramatic power. It is helpful to try to imagine the pace of the show before you start making slides, as this may well influence your choice and style of images.

5. Making images for the show

Clearly the pictures and the words must evolve together.

The title slides are used as part of the story. The first slide simply has the word "LIFE" in large green letters. This is followed quickly by another slide with the same word LIFE but with the words "through death", underneath, as if they are roots, feeding the word "life".

A gentle musical sound-track begins, and a series of slides are then displayed of animals feeding. Each slide of an animal is followed by a close up of the food being eaten.

After a series of such slides, the sound-track interrupts these images by stating that for one life to continue another life must die. The explanation is as short as possible without being obscure.

There then follow a series of slides which show a simple stone altar with fire on the top. This could be shot from a scale model, or, for maximum effect, "on location". In film production the ability to find good locations is highly prized. Either way, to get the most from the time-consuming work, you could shoot pictures from different angles and at different times of day. The changing angles and lighting in this series of slides are a visual device to create a rhythm and shift attention to the commentary.

The commentary mentions some of the Old Testament references

to sacrifice, and stresses that God's rules for sacrifice were quite strict.

The next section of the show has to deal with the reasons for sacrifice and is the most difficult part of the show. It must also form the bridge to the treatment of the cross and the Lord's supper which is to be the climax of the show. Again, the sound-track plays the lead. The images used are of a figure silhouetted on the horizon.

The first is of the figure raking the earth. The sound-track says that everything man has is a gift from God and thus does not truly belong to man.

This is followed by a silhouette of the figure sitting at a table eating. The commentary says that the greatest of all our gifts is life, something worth remembering every meal.

The commentary goes on to say how we are cut off from the source of that gift. Repeat the same image but taken from a substantial distance, with a threatening sky in the background. This could be done by combining two slides in one frame, as the silhouette would effectively mask unwanted portions of a dramatic storm-cloud shot. See page 52–53 on "back projection" for other ways to achieve similar effects.

God ordained sacrifice as a reminder for us of the seriousness of our rebellion. Photo of flames on altar.

But God does not taunt us, and through sacrifice there is restoration. The offerings of the Old Testament were picked up by New Testament writers to explain the significance of Christ's death. The image here is a little tricky, as the table where the figure was sitting is now photographed from a side view with a loaf of bread and a bottle of wine. The composition of the picture forms a kind of cross — not immediately obvious, perhaps.

The following slides move in close to reveal the elements of the communion as the commentary establishes the link.

The result of "feeding on him in our minds", continues the commentary, is that nothing else is more important in our lives. Here images of various possessions, friends, and concerns, are quickly alternated with the earlier picture of the burning altar.

The show concludes with a slide showing Romans 5.9: "By Christ's sacrificial death we are now put right with God . . ."

Even though it has taken quite some space to describe the development of the show in this outline, you will see that there are many details that would need to be worked out in a tight storyboard. For the purposes of this sample only photographs were used, and to execute the treatment well would necessitate some searching for locations, props, etc. It might take three or four rolls of film to get the right shots. The whole programme, described here as an example, might take three or four weeks of your spare time to produce.

This theme is difficult, but by grasping the nettle something quite powerful could emerge. You would be making an innovative contribution to your churches' Easter meditation. Having done it once, you will see hundreds of things that could be improved. You may wish to touch up the show, or you may simply move on to doing another show on a different theme. After the next two sets of Technical tips covering photography, and sound-tracks for slide shows there are some suggested projects for you to try out.

Technical tips... Photography for slide shows

■ When preparing artwork for slides, make sure that you draw up boards which are of the right proportions. Most slide shows use the frame in the horizontal position (called "landscape"), so a good size for the original artwork is eight-by-twelve inches.

■ Remember that white will photograph as clear film. Clear film shows the dirt and is very bright. If you show a series of subdued, moody pictures, and suddenly show a slide which is predominantly white, everyone will be forced to squint. The best way to avoid this is always to work from a pale tonal background. This also allows you to use white as a colour. A grey paper pasted to the board can then have other cut-out shapes applied — a drawing on white paper can be carefully cut out with a scalpel and stuck to this background.

■ Black and white photos have a strong graphic quality, are fairly cheap to produce, and work well in conjunction with colour. From normal black and white negatives it is possible to make so called "contact prints" on a high-contrast graphic arts film, which is available from most larger printers. This film can then be developed in ordinary photographic paper developer, or in a special high-contrast developer. The result is a slide with good dense black, suitable for projection.

Using glass slide mounts, these black and white slides can then be sandwiched together with coloured film, painted, or dyed. You can also combine images with many thin materials: open weave cloth,

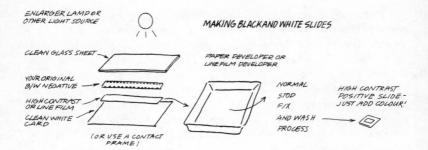

ENLARGER LAMP OR
OTHER LIGHT SOURCE

CLEAN GLASS SHEET

YOUR ORIGINAL
B/W NEGATIVE

HIGH CONTRAST
OR LINE FILM

CLEAN WHITE
CARD

(OR USE A CONTACT
FRAME)

PAPER DEVELOPER OR
LINE FILM DEVELOPER

NORMAL
STOP
FIX
AND WASH
PROCESS

HIGH CONTRAST
POSITIVE SLIDE –
JUST ADD COLOUR!

coloured tissue-paper, hand-painted acetate, even thin wood-shavings. These devices should be used sparingly for best effect.

■ If you plan to apply text to any of your slides, it is best to use Letraset or any equivalent transfer type. Unless you are very good at hand lettering you will discover that enlargement makes hand drawn lettering forms look quite scruffy. For making title slides, it is possible to Letraset directly on to an overhead projector slide (an acetate), and then cut the acetate to fit a slide mount. Of course you can also Letraset directly on to a pale slide. In general, though, it is better to use white lettering on a dark backgroud. There are several ways to achieve this: as described above, high-contrast black and white film can be used to photograph normal black-on-white lettering, and then be developed in paper-developer; or transfer lettering on film can be contacted on to film to produce a reversal. By sandwiching coloured overhead projector film with this negative, the result is lettering in colour.

■ You can make reasonably convincing backgrounds for presentation slides by projecting a slide on to a screen and re-photographing it with an actor or object in front. Hang a smooth, white sheet in the middle of a room and put the slide projector on one side, the actor or object on the other. Position the actor far enough away from the screen to ensure that the image on the screen doesn't make a pronounced edge-lighting on the actor. If you place your camera directly in line with the projector, the resulting photo can look very convincing — someone standing in front of the Alps, for instance. This technique can also be used to add scenes-out-the-window to interior shots.

■ Photograph your artwork in even daylight (not sunlight) and make certain that the film plane is perfectly parallel with the artwork.

52

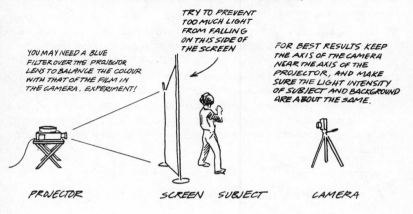

SETTING UP REAR PROJECTION SHOTS

YOU MAY NEED A BLUE FILTER OVER THE PROJECTOR LENS TO BALANCE THE COLOUR WITH THAT OF THE FILM IN THE CAMERA. EXPERIMENT!

TRY TO PREVENT TOO MUCH LIGHT FROM FALLING ON THIS SIDE OF THE SCREEN

FOR BEST RESULTS KEEP THE AXIS OF THE CAMERA NEAR THE AXIS OF THE PROJECTOR, AND MAKE SURE THE LIGHT INTENSITY OF SUBJECT AND BACKGROUND ARE ABOUT THE SAME.

PROJECTOR   SCREEN   SUBJECT   CAMERA

It is best to shoot all the slides in the same session, and have the film developed at the same time. This helps to eliminate annoying changes in image density and colour hues. Consult a book on copy-photography such as that published by Kodak, for more detailed information. Better still, find someone else to do it for you!

Technical tips... A sound-track for a slide show

■ The easiest sound-track to make is with a narrator and pre-recorded music.

■ For special effects and a more professional result you may wish to mix all kinds of sounds . . . As the picture of the gull comes on the screen, the sound of a gull's cry fades to the sound of the sea . . . Great, but how are you going to do it? Probably not by taking your stereo tape-deck to Brighton. For this kind of sound effect it is best to use a "library" record. There is an inexpensive series produced by the BBC. They may even be in your local library.

■ If you can tape some of your own effects, so much the better, but care must be taken when mixing the sound to keep an even sound level. As this is a book on the visual, not aural arts, the intricacies of sound-mixing will be left out. You should be able to find an able collaborator.

■ If your show will be shown publicly, check on music and sound effects copyright with the publisher.

■ Try the sound with the images again and again, until you are satisfied that they work well together. This has the added benefit of helping you to develop the timing for slide-changes that will make the presentation a success. There are a number of electronically controlled units on the market which can do it all for you, but these are quite expensive. Most work with two projectors and allow for dissolves and other tricks. Very nice if you can manage to hire one. But a single projector and tape-deck can still make an excellent impression.

 Slide show

Here are two different ideas for you to try out.

1. The race

The image of a race is used by various New Testament writers to teach about Christian life. They had in mind the ancient world's equivalent of our own athletics meetings. This is a rich image to explore.

■ What can you find out about the ancient games?

■ What is the modern attitude to fast runners and successful athletes?

■ How does our modern concern with "jogging" and fitness compare with a Christian's "race of faith"?

The key passages to explore to start with are 1 Corinthians 9.23–37; 1 Timothy 6.11–16; 2 Timothy 2.3–7 and 4.6–8; and Hebrews 11.1—12.2.

Set yourself a target of a three-to-five minute slide show to help your own congregation reflect upon the meaning of this image, to be used around the time of some major televised athletics meeting such as the Olympic games or the European or Commonwealth games.

2. Illustrating a song

For some of you the main interest in a slide show will be the excitement of finding or taking the pictures. You may therefore prefer to start with a fixed sound-track, and simply set out to illustrate that sound-track.

Some possible sources of a sound-track:

- A rock song
- A song which sets a well-known Bible passage to music
- A good reading of a passage from the Bible on tape

Try, for example, the song from "Sing Good News — The Musical" entitled "Arise Jerusalem" (published by Bible Society). This song is based on one of Isaiah's prophecies concerning the return of God's people from exile. Slides from your own or someone else's tour of the Holy Land might well be useful. And not only historical ones, but ones that reflect the rich culture of modern-day Israel.

Set out by exploring the lyrics of the song just as you would any other Bible passage. Look for the context, and try to find what the writer was wanting to convey. Then choose pictures to help communicate that message.

The advantage of using a fixed sound-track is, of course, that you can concentrate on just one part of the creative process described in the worked example — i.e. the image-making process.

Banners for the church

Church halls are like people. Some are withdrawn and cool, others gushy and over dramatic. Like people, too, we tend to judge an environment at a glance and stick to our opinion. Although you may not be given a free hand (or budget) to totally refurbish the church, you may well be able to enhance the space through selective decorations, such as banners. Annual festivals such as Christmas, Easter, Pentecost, and Harvest; a special series of talks etc., are ideal occasions for creating and hanging banners.

Banners can be as elaborate or simple as you care to make them. You may have a group of retired seamstresses ready to stitch your every sketch, or you may have a struggle to find someone with a sewing machine. No matter, there are methods of banner making which will suit.

Worked example... **Banners**

As an example, take one of the themes from the Psalms. This is an easy task because the psalms are full of proclamations of praise — a very suitable theme for the "public speech" of banners. Assume that your theme will be one of the meditations from that great reflection on the words and word of God, Psalm 19. We tend to see God's creation as distinct from his salvation. In Psalm 19, the psalmist parallels God's glory as revealed in nature with the beauty of God's commands for our lives. Both reveal the perfection of his ways.

God's Glory in Creation

How clearly the sky reveals God's glory!
How plainly it shows what he has done!
²Each day announces it to the following day;
 each night repeats it to the next.
³No speech or words are used,
 no sound is heard;
⁴yet their message goes out to all the world
 and is heard to the ends of the earth.
God made a home in the sky for the sun;
⁵ it comes out in the morning like a happy bridegroom,
 like an athlete eager to run a race.
⁶It starts at one end of the sky
 and goes across to the other.
 Nothing can hide from its heat.

The Law of the LORD

⁷The law of the LORD is perfect;
 it gives new strength.
The commands of the LORD are trustworthy,
 giving wisdom to those who lack it.

⁸The laws of the LORD are right,
 and those who obey them are happy.
The commands of the LORD are just and give understanding to the mind.
⁹Reverence for the LORD is good;
 it will continue for ever.
The judgements of the LORD are just;
 they are always fair.
¹⁰They are more desirable than the finest gold;
 they are sweeter than the purest honey
¹¹They give knowledge to me,
 your servant;
 I am rewarded for obeying them.

¹²No one can see his own errors;
 deliver me, LORD, from hidden faults!
¹³Keep me safe, also, from wilful sins;
 don't let them rule over me.
Then I shall be perfect
 and free from the evil of sin.

¹⁴May my words and my thoughts be acceptable to you,
 O LORD, my refuge and my redeemer!

(Psalm 19)

Read through the passage. Highlight any phrases that you feel are particularly significant. Then, in another coloured pen, mark any phrases or verses which sum up the theme of the Psalm "God's glory in creation".

For the purposes of this worked example let's select part of verse 9 to work with: "Reverence for the LORD is good; it will continue for ever" and aim to develop a banner that conveys a mood rather than tells a story. The mood is worship, worship that continues from the beginning of time, to the end of time — "for ever".

The first and last letter of the Hebrew alphabet, "alpha" (A) and "omega" (Ω), are used because of their symbolism of "beginning" and "end".

The text is integrated into these two graphic elements.

The typographic style selected is a modern interpretation of the old brush-drawn calligraphy of the medieval church. The result has a taste of both old and new styles, and a restrained decorative quality that would fit well in almost any environment.

The materials are felt, except for the alpha and omega characters. These are silk, which is very slightly filled through the back of the banner so as to give them a subtle relief effect.

Banner making

■ Whereas drawings and slides are seen only momentarily, banners are usually made for longer periods of display. This means that they need to be integrated into the surroundings and that they may have to be rather robustly constructed. In some halls, banners can have an important acoustical effect; if speakers always sound like they are at the back of a cave, banners might help.

■ Banners are normally made of cloth. They can be sewn, painted, or both. Designing a banner is somewhat different from doing a drawing, as designs must take account of the nature of cloth.

■ Make a series of sketches until you are happy with the composition, and then a final full-scale drawing which can be used as a guide for assembly.

■ The process is quite "low-tech" compared with some of the other techniques in this book. Cloth, often felt, is cut out to the desired shape and sewn to a backing cloth. When cutting out fine forms (such as letters) cloth has the frustrating inclination to stretch and fray. This is further aggravated when it comes to sewing all the bits together. One way round this is to spray the back of the cloth with adhesive and stick the cloth to a light paper. This will provide a stable base for trimming and sewing. The paper won't be seen in the finished banner.

■ To cut complicated shapes with accuracy it is better to use a scalpel than scissors. Change the blade often, and you will find that it will cut the cloth/paper combination very cleanly.

■ For temporary banners there are heavy duty spray adhesives which will hold with remarkable tenacity. This eliminates the sewing altogether. A light coating of adhesive can be very useful in trying out shapes in different positions.

■ It is possible to make banners in relief. Felt is quite a pliant material. When wet it can be stretched over a form, and allowed to dry. When dry it will retain the new shape, which can be filled with granulated foam, kapok, or other fillers. If one object on a banner is in relief, the effect can be very dramatic.

Banners

Many people have used the Annie Vallotton illustrations to be found in most *Good News Bibles*, as the basis for a simple banner. The bold economy of her illustrations make them ideal for adaptation.

For instance, see what you can make of one of the following illustrations. Particularly note how you will use the three components — texture of material, colour, and relief — to add to the effect of the illustrations.

I will praise you, LORD — Psalm 9.1

Clap your hands for joy — Psalm 47.1

I saw the Spirit come down like a dove — John 1.32

Backdrops

For a mission, a special children's week, or some drama production, you may be called on to make a backdrop, an environment, or a "set". For this you will need the help of other people. If you are responsible for the design, remember to take account of the physical structure of the building, and where the backdrop will be used. Don't paint scenes in poster paint if they are to be hung out of doors; don't hang huge expanses of canvas on thin string; don't overrate the power of sticky tape, etc. Backdrops can be painted on paper or canvas, but either must be well-secured. A twelve-foot square of paper can weigh a lot!

Have at least two people check all fixings to the fabric of the building. If you are asked to build anything which people are to climb on, this is doubly important. Remember, too, that your construction is quite likely to be the centre of attention for children, even if no one is minding them. Make your constructions safe.

Technical tips... **Backdrops and stage painting**

■ Assuming that the biggest painting you have ever made is smaller than a stage backdrop, there will be a number of obstacles to overcome in addition to the structural difficulties. It is unlikely that you will be able to try your design in a full-scale preliminary sketch, and it is probable that you will need help with the painting itself. This means that you must be able to visualize the finished effect and guide others.

■ The simplest way to do this is to make slides from fairly large sketches (use cheap "lining paper" stuck together to make a six-by-four foot sheet). These sketches can be made as an intermediate phase between your sketchbook drawings and the final painting.

■ If you are after a realistic effect, such as a view of the Sea of Galilee, you may be able to simply project a slide on to the canvas. The shapes are drawn on to the canvas with a charcoal pencil. *Don't* use felt-tipped pens as this can bleed through the final layer of paint. You will need a strong line to work to.

■ Figures and faces are more difficult, and may require turning the projector back on after the tracing stage in order to paint the forms in.

PAINTED CANVAS BACKDROP FOR A CHURCH ENTRANCE -
USED DURING A CHILDREN'S MISSION. THE CHILDREN LIKED
THE FACT THAT ADULTS HAD TO DUCK TO GET IN !

PHOTO CREDIT: MOYRA MORRIS

61

■ You will need to monitor the progress by viewing occasionally from the back of the hall. The easiest way to paint a backdrop is by painting it flat on the floor, as you won't need stepladders or scaffolding. However, it is easier to see what you are doing if you work vertically. Take your pick!

■ It may take a while to get the knack of a broad handling of the paint. This is important, both to maintain an overall evenness, and to save time. For trees, landscapes, mountains, and other large forms, it sometimes helps to tie a brush to the end of a three-or-four foot pole. This prevents intricate fiddling and lets you see the work from some distance. Cut-down paint rollers are also useful. What looks huge to the painter may look fairly insignificant once the backdrop is in place.

■ Stay with slightly muted colours if possible, as this prevents the backdrop from conflicting with the action taking place in front of it. A few spots of more intense colour added near the end of the painting can help liven the surface if it appears dull. Coloured chalks come in handy for this, too.

■ Images can be combined on the same surface by using a number of slides for different areas of the painting. This should be used with great care, as it is quite difficult to visualize how different elements may work together. However, some unusual effects can be achieved by overlapping images and painting with thinned paint. This "show-through" can permit several forms to be combined for a coherent graphic effect — such as a variety of plant, animal, and land forms for a series of talks on creation.

■ Canvas purchased from a canvas merchant (rather than the local art-supply shop) is very cheap, and can be obtained in wall-sized pieces. This canvas should be primed with a pale matt emulsion. When dry it can be painted with emulsion or acrylic paints.

■ Foam paint rollers can be "engraved" by snipping with scissors or by careful application of a soldering iron. The textures which result can provide an interesting base-layer for subsequent painting. It is quite easy to get marble, stone, or grass textures.

■ One of the advantages of canvas is that the same canvas can be reprimed and painted almost indefinitely. Put out a call to your friends for any old emulsion paint and you will have materials to last many years. Alternatively, you can purchase powdered colour and mix it with water and a little vinyl wallpaper paste. This is a very economical medium.

■ A well-painted backdrop can enhance an environment or totally change it. By virtue of the sheer size of a backdrop an atmosphere of anticipation is created. If you wish to get the maximum dramatic effect from your work, consider installing hidden spot-or-flood-lights to illuminate it.

Of course, the prime use of such theatrical settings is for dramatic productions. A good stage-set can help the morale of actors and give pleasure to everyone. You may not get many opportunities to paint on such a large scale. If you do, it is worth looking at a book on stage painting — some of the tricks of the trade are quite ingenious.

The most effective backdrop isn't always the most elaborate. The illustration shows one used by Footprints Threatre Company adaptable for use in street theatre, reviews, churches — almost anywhere.

A simple backdrop used by Footprints Theatre Co.

Murals

Group murals are a festive project. People get in each other's way, have to share materials, and debate the best arrangements of elements. This activity particularly excites children, but interesting results are likely with any group.

You can use an interior or exterior wall.

Technical tips... **Murals**

■ If you don't want the mural to be a permanent feature, stretch lining-paper or any other roll-paper along a large smooth wall.

■ You may want to plan the murals from drawings made by individuals. These drawings can be photographed on to slide-film, projected, and filled in by the person who did the original drawing. This enlargement technique produces dynamic murals because the scale of the individual drawing is maintained. A crayon-line grows to a bold inch-thick stroke. Try to preserve as much of the quality of the original as you can.

■ A slide-projector can also be used as a light-source for tracing off silhouettes, or for projecting pictures to be traced. If you can find a slide-projector that is equipped with a zoom lens, this makes it easy to vary the size of objects.

■ A rhythm can be given to the overall mural by repeating certain elements. If you have a good slide of a tree, for instance, this can be projected onto the paper in different places, and painted in by different participants.

■ Poster paints are the cheapest form of colour for such large-scale works, but they are rather fragile. If applied too thickly the paint will crack and fall off. Adhesion can be improved by the addition of vinyl wallpaper paste. Paint rollers can also be used to good effect, particularly if you have some in a variety of widths. Whatever materials you choose, take the precaution of covering everything in the space with tarpaulins!

■ If you want an exterior mural to last, be sure to use oil-based paint. There are special light-fast paints made expressly for exterior murals.

■ Many of the technical tips for backdrops and stage-painting can also be useful when doing murals. The difference between a mural and a backdrop is in use, as a backdrop usually is intended to create an environment for a specific event. But there is nothing to prevent you from using paper murals as a form of decoration for the church. Once you have made a mural you will find that enthusiasm will be contagious.

Try it out... A group mural

The mural gives you the chance to experiment with bold and adventurous themes. You may want to give the six days of creation a miss, but some of the grander epics of Old Testament history — the parting of the Red Sea, the fall of Jericho, Nehemiah rebuilding the Jerusalem walls, will keep you profitably occupied for a long while.

Better still, explore one large theme, such as the life of the early church in Acts, and incorporate into your mural as many aspects of the subject as possible. In this respect, the mural which can pull together diverse and contradictory elements into a single image is a close kin to the way the Bible expresses its truth. The Bible gives many different views on a single truth, and it is only by collecting them all together that we can begin to grasp the whole.

Below is the beginning of a biblical data-base from which you can begin a mural on the life of the early church. One way of approaching this list, for group work, is to pair off, and give one subject or passage to each pair for them to work on ideas which can be included in the mural.

The coming of the Holy Spirit	Acts 2
The believers share their possessions	Acts 4.32–37
Ananias and Sapphira	Acts 5.1–11
The stoning of Stephen	Acts 7.54 — 8.1
The conversion of Saul	Acts 9.1–25
Peter and Cornelius	Acts 10
In prison at Philippi	Acts 16.16–40
The riot in Ephesus	Acts 19.21–41
Paul visits James	Acts 21.17–26
Paul sails for Rome	Acts 27
In Malta	Acts 28.1–10

Conclusion

If you've tried some of the previous exercises, you will have discovered how the enthusiasm and alertness of one or two individuals can radically alter attitudes to the arts of a church as a whole. We all run the risk of lethargy. The word worship means "service". We usually think of coming to the Sunday service to "get something to take away". Why not instead come to serve and be of service?

The imaginative use of visual material and the imaginative exploration of the Bible can indeed help in church life. But that is not all. By donating your gifts to God and the local church, your artistic interest and skills could be used by God to help the whole church become more alive and active. An active church will grow. Surprise, surprise — the artist can help here, too.

5. Christian publicity

This chapter is for anyone involved in Christian publicity. Many products, services, and causes in our culture are evaluated on the basis of the publicity which they produce. Some may lament the superficiality of our "ad" age, but like it or not, many of our opinions are formed by the images we see. Christian publicity rarely seems to match the quality or power of these secular sales-pitches. The aim of this chapter is to encourage you to use your artistic interests to help attract others to the gospel. The gospel is not "a product", of course, but there may be some advantage in initially presenting it as such. We have a claim to make — Christ *really* is the opportunity for a new life.

A publicity project

The most important context for our Christian publicity is the message of our own lives. If the world sees Christians they respect, that will have a major effect on whether they listen to what we say. So most of us will try to be tactful, imaginative, and honest in the presence of non-believers. Yet Christian publicity is another matter. Insensitive tracts, badly-produced brochures, and cluttered, jargon-filled magazines are the norm. That God can use some of the things prepared in his name is a testimony to his power, not to the thought Christians have given the matter. Think of the effort and concern which accompanies any wedding announcement — should God have less?

Fortunately, in recent years many Christians have been stirred out of their sleepwalk and have begun to produce well-written, attractive materials. Such publicity not only works, but shows that we take our own message seriously. Not a bad thing.

Posters and leaflets are not the only Christian publicity. Local radio, events, personal contact, newspapers, are all important, but almost all Christian groups need printed publicity — whether tracts, leaflets, programme cards, invitations for a series of lectures, posters, or church newspapers — at some time. Someone has to make these things, either by being dragged into it or, as in your case, by volunteering with a great show of enthusiasm!

The level of your involvement in publicity can vary from doing the occasional poster for a coffee morning to handling all aspects of a group's publicity. For students in university, polytechnic, or college, it will probably be the latter. For any groups concerned with evangelism, the post of publicity officer is a key position.

A tough job

It would be easy to list the requirements of a publicity officer in such a way that no one would want the job; for there is no avoiding the fact that handling publicity means dashing about and wrestling with schedules and budgets. However, enormous satisfaction comes from seeing publicity bring results.

Developing good publicity to serve evangelistic goals is not easy, which is one of the reasons that there are few good models to copy. One needs not only a good grasp of the Bible but an ability to understand the non-believer's reaction.

The ten commandments, the miracles of Jesus, phrases such as "The children of Israel", — such things are "familiar" to many people brought up in western culture. But the knowledge is a weak confused thing with no framework, acquired by a process of handed-down mis-quotes. To make sensible statements about the Bible it is often necessary to clear up a host of misunderstandings.

It is crucial that you avoid saying things that only Christians would understand. It can be helpful to show that you realize that most people feel that Christianity "doesn't work", or is for "another kind of person". You must listen to the views of the person you wish to listen to your "views". Be prepared to see that some of the things you believe may not be an accurate reflection of the teaching of the Bible. Above all, do not present the message in a fashion which condemns readers before they have had a chance to read.

Theologians use the word "apologetics" to describe the process whereby the gospel is defended by reason and argument. The mental associations of this term are sometimes visible in an apologetic attitude to expressing our faith. We are on the defensive, apologising for the awkward, complex system of belief with which we are burdened. The best antidote to this shy "so sorry" approach is to reread the story of the early church in the book of Acts. There we find the characteristics which will give the balance we need in the task of presenting the gospel: boldness, dedication, familiarity with the material, cultural sensitivity, continual prayer . . .

Strategy

■ Discuss strategy with others.

■ Read books and develop an eye for publicity materials.

■ Learn to ask questions of other publicity you see: How does it work? What is the audience? What issues are raised?

■ In your own Bible study, ask the same questions, and others: How could the ideas be translated into a form that would catch the attention of people you know?

The strategic thinking required to plan an effective publicity "campaign" will force you to define your objectives as clearly as is possible. The most common publicity objective is to get people along to a meeting. But there is no reason why publicity can't also be used to provoke questions, or to interest people in reading the Bible themselves. These latter objectives are covered in the second section of this chapter — a poster campaign.

How about the first?

Worked example... A publicity project

Imagine that you are a student and that a guest speaker is coming to the polytechnic to do a series of evangelistic talks called "Jesus in the twentieth century". You bravely promise to handle the publicity and everyone sighs with relief. "That takes care of that!" they think.

"What about the budget?" you ask.

"For what? oh, yes . . . the posters. How much will it cost?"

Now you're stuck. If you pick a figure out of the blue, everyone will remind you of it when you are over budget. If you ask for a realistic figure straight away, the others will panic. So don't give a figure until you have done your sums.

Now down to work. The steps outlined in some detail below are fairly typical for most publicity projects, whether in churches, colleges, schools, or community. To spread the load, choose a group of three or four others to help.

1. Define the purpose

Whom do you hope to attract to the meetings? At what age-group are the talks aimed? How will the talks be backed up, if at all? How will publicity be distributed? How many people would you realistically expect to come? How many came the last time such an event was sponsored? Time spent at this early stage will help focus energy where it is needed.

2. Determine the items

You will need a leaflet or handbill at least. A poster which has the same image as the handbill would be a boost. A sign needs to be displayed at the venue. With finance in mind, prepare two lists, one for the minimum publicity, and another showing the items which you think would really help attract people to the talks.

3. Estimate the quantities

Will the handbill be deposited through letterboxes, left in the cafeteria, handed out in the car park, or all of the above? This is likely to be educated guess-work on your first attempt. You may be able to find out what other groups have done in the past.

Get assurance of help in distribution at this stage. It is no use having two thousand beautiful handbills if no one is around when they are to be given out. The average rate of response to materials put "cold" through a letterbox is less than one percent. For something which looks "religious" the rate is even lower. On the other hand, personal distribution might gain a return as high as three or four percent.

4. Make a schedule

Assume that you have decided that: (1) you are primarily trying to reach other students in the polytechnic; and that (2) you will need five hundred leaflets and one hundred posters. These items will take some time to prepare and print. You must establish deadlines for (1) finishing the artwork; (2) getting the results printed; and (3) distribution. Be realistic.

5. Exploring the Bible

In your preparations, explore the theme of the talks yourself. It is too easy to take a title as a starting point and construct a whole publicity campaign around it. Contact the speaker and discuss the content of his talks. Study the references he mentions. For many people Jesus belongs to the past. He is honoured in the same way that other "historic" figures are regarded — Aristotle and King Arthur have also made contributions to our culture. Yet the Bible doesn't regard Jesus as just a teacher or king. The first chapter of Colossians, verses 15–23 is a beautiful and powerful description of the person and work of Christ. We read:

The Person and Work of Christ

[15]Christ is the visible likeness of the invisible God. He is the first-born Son, superior to all created things. [16]For through him God created everything in heaven and on earth, the seen and the unseen things, including spiritual powers, lords, rulers, and authorities. God created the whole universe through him and for him. [17]Christ existed before all things, and in union with him all things have their proper place. [18]He is the head of his body, the church; he is the source of the body's life. He is the first-born Son, who was raised from death, in order that he alone might have the first place in all things. [19]For it was by God's own decision that the Son has in himself the full nature of God. [20]Through the Son, then, God decided to bring the whole universe back to himself. God made peace through his Son's sacrificial death on the cross and so brought back to himself all things, both on earth and in heaven. [21]At one time you were far away from God and were his enemies because of the evil things you did and thought. [22]But now, by means of the physical death of his Son, God has made you his friends, in order to bring you, holy, pure, and faultless, into his presence. [23]You must, of course, continue faithful on a firm and sure foundation, and must not allow yourselves to be shaken from the hope you gained when you heard the gospel. It is of this gospel that I, Paul, became a servant—this gospel which has been preached to everybody in the world.

(Colossians 1.15–23)

What would you need to say to convey these same statements in the language of the twentieth century? How can we get across that the whole of creation and the forms by which we organize society have their source in Christ, that everything there is has its goal in him?

These grand, sweeping descriptions are difficult to fully comprehend, much less express in a poster. However, study of the nature and activity of Christ leads us to the unmistakable conclusion that there isn't anyone, anything, any condition which is more important than Christ. How can this extravagent Jesus have bearing on our humble affairs?

First, by reminding us that we are near-sighted. We focus only on the tiny patch of experience before us, we hear only the strident voices of our own hasty age. The long scale from the beginning of time to eternity beyond doesn't get a look in. Second, if Jesus is the maker of all things, he has every right to specify how those things are to be used. Everything, ourselves included, is his property. Finally, Jesus is relevant for today because his offer of salvation extends to the twentieth century. The apostles and disciples expected Jesus to return within their own life-times. He didn't, and innumerable "experts" since have attempted to predict the day. This extended period — the time from Christ's words, "It is finished" to the present day, is witness to God's grace. He has "held history open" that more people might meet him.

So the relevance of Jesus in the twentieth century is total, supreme. Such a perspective won't be welcomed with open arms by the unbeliever, and your publicity can't possibly convey every nuance. But your design has a better chance of being effective if you yourself are alive to the issues you are promoting.

6. The creative part

If the title of the series is fixed, it probably should feature prominently in your publicity. On the other hand, you may not think that "Jesus in the twentieth century" is a particularly dynamic title for people brought up on rock-groups with names like "Mashed Aspirin" or "Rubber Kneecaps".

Get together with one or two friends and toss ideas around. Remember that you are trying to change people's perception that Jesus is irrelevant. Somewhat enigmatic or slangy titles can be effective: "Jesus — why the system nailed him", "The teacher who made the world talk", "The force explains . . ." Go ahead and get carried away at this point. Loose your loony, absurd, and shocking ideas. Write them all down. Good ideas are often embedded in crazy comments. Work in bursts of forty minutes or so, followed by a break. Sooner or later you'll hit the jackpot, or at least it will feel like it. If you are in charge of publicity you are ready for the next stage. Otherwise get your idea approved. Show your three best titles to half-a-dozen people, and get their comment.

Now before we go on to the next stage, a few comments on copy-writing.

 **Publicity copy-writing**

In your planning sessions you will have undoubtedly discussed images as well as titles — we can't help flitting between pictures and words. As both pictures and text must work together, you will want to find some bright spark with a stunning turn of phrase. Yourself perhaps? Whoever writes the text would do well to bear a few basic points in mind:

■ Keep sentences short, but vary the length.

■ Don't "explain away" the meeting. You are trying to get people to come, not feel that they've already been.

■ Don't threaten or patronize your readers. "You are headed for hell unless . . ." or "Are you lost and depressed?" are not good copy-lines.

■ Try to put yourself in your reader's army boots, jogging shoes, or phosphorescent socks. What would your non-Christian friends say to their friends if they were discussing your copy?

■ Bite the bullet and show your copy to one of the aforementioned non-Christian friends. Let them read it before you explain what you meant to say. Ask them if it works.

Write as you would write to someone you respect. By all means use wit and humour, but avoid complex jumps in thought designed to let you fit in another joke.

Brainstorms and thumbnails

If you have a strong-enough copy-line it is possible that you may not need a visual image, or only a very small one. But for the purpose of the following discussion, assume that at the last moment you hear that the speaker insists on the original title, "Jesus in the twentieth century". And you had such a *perfect* one lined up . . . take heart. It happens all the time. Concentrate on finding the appropriate image.

Take your A4 sketchbook, and make ten or twelve rectangles

approximately 2 inches by 1½ inches ("A" proportions). A rectangular window cut from card makes it easy to quickly cover the page with rectangles. This allows you to try out ideas in what designers call "thumbnail sketches". You can freely experiment with different layouts of text and images, and have the entire record of your thinking on a few pages. Drawings in your concept book which were rejected for one project might come in handy later. As you draw, write notes next to the drawings. This is particularly valuable when you look back on them after some time. It is good practice to do a few further sketches after you have come up with "the solution".

So, after several cups of coffee, five-hundred yards of pacing, and three visits to the fridge, your paper will look something like the one on the page opposite.

Your choice of which of these to develop is partly instinctive, and partly governed by the form of printing you will be using, and your budget.

The "Last Supper" idea could be quite effective, but you would have to find a good reproduction of the painting, and stacks of magazines to search and snip for the figures. Finding figures in appropriate positions might prove difficult. To really do justice to this concept it should be printed in "half-tones" (see page 76), and this involves extra expense. This "solution" would cost considerable time and money. One down.

The computer-screen design might be a little confusing. Scratch two. The telephone hot-line to Jesus is trite, so knock it on the head. And so you proceed, always trying to evaluate **potential impact**, **suitability for the audience**, and **work involved**. The decisions which would take pages to describe happen quite quickly in practice — you soon condense the raw ideas to no more than three possible solutions. It can be helpful to have the comments of other people, but as at this stage your precious idea is a mere scribble, others might not be able to see how it would work.

At last you settle for idea number eight, the engraving with the microphone. You select this because it will be fairly easy to put together, it will reproduce well, and it has the right elements of humour and mild surprise to suit the intended audience. After all, the tame, sentimental pictures of Jesus from the last century are the epitome of the irrelevance many people would associate with our faith. By putting a microphone in front of such a picture, the design seems to acknowledge the improbability of Christ speaking today. The image is intriguing.

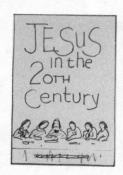

Thumbnail sketches: Jesus in the twentieth century.

You now need to turn the concept into suitable artwork. Let's go through these technical stages in detail.

 Preparing artwork

■ *References*

The first step is to find the reference materials. A suitable old engraving might be found in your grandmother's Bible, or in a book of old religious drawings. If you know what it is that you are looking for (and in this case you do), you can ask others to help you look. The microphone could be drawn, or be a photo. Whatever you decide, it is important to select the images first as they will determine the whole design.

■ *Line and half-tone*

Once located, the images must be converted into a form suitable for the printer. Here it is important to distinguish between "line" artwork and "half-tone" artwork. The former is anything which is black and white with no intermediate grey tones. The text in this book is "line", as are some of the illustrations. "Half-tone" refers to material which has a range of grey tones, such as a photograph.

In order for a range of grey tones to be printed, they must be "screened" (broken down into a grid of dots). This adds cost.

■ *Enlargements and reductions, the versatile PMT*

PMT stands for Photo Mechanical Transfer, but just remember the initials. A PMT is one of the most useful tools of the graphic designer, for it can quickly make lettering any size, or convert small, pale engravings into large, chunky images.

Before having the engraving enlarged, do a full-scale layout for the poster and leaflet. A pantograph is useful for making a rough enlargement of the images to determine position. Assume that the poster will be A3, and the leaflet A5 (hence both of the same proportions). The poster will have the title, image, speaker's name, venue, and date. The leaflet will have all of these, plus about one-hundred words of text. Get the text typed out on a plain white sheet and be very sure that it contains no errors. Let's suppose that the text will be set by an IBM typesetting machine (see below).

Select the type-style for the title from a catalogue of transfer lettering. Buy the sheets in the sizes you will need, or buy the largest sheet which contains both upper and lower-case letters. If you choose the latter, you will then have to have PMTs made to enlarge or reduce the type-sizes.

■ Typesetting

In some publicity hand-lettering can be ideal. A crisp "cartoonist" letter-form done with pen or brush has a casual, friendly look. Other forms of hand-lettering are considerably more difficult. Unless you are an experienced signwriter it is advisable to use transfer-lettering sheets for all headline lettering.

Most publicity requires typesetting. The typewriter, the simplest form of setting, is only appropriate for church newsletters, prayer bulletins, and the like. Use a single-strike carbon ribbon on a smooth cartridge paper for the best results. If you have access to a word processor with a daisywheel printer, so much the better. Dot matrix printers generally are not suitable.

The next step up in quality is typesetting by a special IBM "golfball" machine called the Selectric Composer. Although it is essentially a typewriter, it spaces letters proportionally. Only one proof is provided. Treat it with care. There is usually a minimum charge for IBM setting which makes it expensive to buy a small amount of setting.

Film-setting is superior to IBM and therefore more costly. One advantage of film-setting is that there is generally a good range of type-faces, and these can be set much larger than with the IBM.

■ Marking up

You will need a few basic tools if you wish to determine accurately how the finished setting will look: a calculator, some tracing paper, a type depth-scale (available from a graphic arts shop), and a specimen sheet of the type-face you wish to use. First, count the characters in the text. This can be simplified by drawing a vertical line down the right hand edge of the paragraphs at a point representative of the average line length (as on page 79). Count the characters to this point, including the spaces, and multiply by the number of lines. Suppose the result is 1,250 characters.

Next, measure the width of the space you want the type to fill in your leaflet — say columns of seventy millimetres wide. Hold your ruler against the specimen sheet for the type-size you want, and count the number of characters which fit in seventy millimetres. For instance if you are using 12pt Garamond, there will be about forty-five characters in each line. Divide the total number of characters (1,250) by characters per line (45) and you get 27.75 — thus 28 lines of 12pt Garamond.

Now look on the type depth-scale, and measure the space you want between lines. If you tick off twenty-eight marks on the 12pt scale, the type will be set "solid". It is normal practice to put a little more space between lines — called "leading" from the days when thin lead strips were inserted between metal lines of type. If you measure against the 14pt gauge, the type would have 2pt leading. Write the type-size and total space for each line as a fraction, followed by name of typeface and column width i.e. "12/14 point Garamond × 70mm". It is easier than it sounds.

■ *Artwork for print*

Having selected the type-face, found your engraving, and made the drawing of the microphone, you are ready to have PMTs made by a printer or photographer.

PMTs are charged per "shot", so it pays to combine material which will have the same degree of enlargement or reduction. You can fit images quite closely together, as you will be cutting up the final print. To "mark-up" for a PMT, draw a line just outside the image area and write the measurement that you want the line to appear on the finished PMT. Or, rather than getting in trouble with your grandmother for writing in her Bible, make a simple tracing and indicate, for instance, that the distance across the shoulders of the figure is to come up to 130mm for one print (the poster), and 60mm for the second (the leaflet). If you are fortunate, the printer or photographer will make PMTs while you wait. Usually you will be told that the PMTs will be ready the next day.

Meanwhile, prepare the board on which all of the components will be pasted down — a stiff white card about six inches larger all-round than the finished poster. With a sharp pale-blue pencil (a pale-blue line won't pick up on the printing-plate) draw the A3 rectangle.

If there is any transfer lettering which appears the same size on the finished poster as on the sheets you have purchased, you can set it on a clean piece of typing paper and paste it in position on the artwork. Again, you will find it helpful to draw a pale-blue reference line. Aerosol adhesives are very convenient, if expensive. If you

AVERAGE
LINE
LENGTH

12 point
High quality layout typesetting or complicated jobbing work – the Linotronic is ideally suited for both. Sophisticated advertisements and complicated tabular work can be composed as 〈7 easily as scientific work and special forms. Rules

13 point
1/2 mro 10 . 20 mm 30 40 . 50 60 .70 .80

FIND OUT HOW MANY CHARACTERS
OF THE SELECTED TYPEFACE WILL
FIT IN THE DESIRED WIDTH.

10½	11	11½	12	12½	13	13½	14
10½ PTS.	11 PTS.	11½ PTS.	12 PTS.	12½ PTS.	13 PTS.	13½ PTS.	14 PTS.

Depth scale
Geliot Whitman
01-699 9262

A DEPTH SCALE –
USED TO DETERMINE
HOW MUCH SPACE
TYPESET COPY
WILL FILL.

79

make a mistake in the lettering it is possible to remove the offending letter by dabbing it with the sticky side of a bit of masking tape.

Assemble the PMTs and type-setting in a similar manner. Try to keep the artwork clean and all of the bits well-stuck-down and square. If there is a stray fleck of black on the PMT it can be removed by lightly scratching with the tip of a scalpel.

Check the artwork again for mis-spellings, lines that aren't straight, and damaged transfer-type. Also check that the date, time, venue, etc., are all correct! When you are satisfied, cover the artwork with a sheet of tracing paper hinged at the top with masking tape, and write on this overlay the details of ink colour, number of copies to be printed, and paper-type. From your discussions with the printer you should have a good idea of the sort of paper you want.

Your artwork, in the printer's term, is now "camera ready". Printing usually takes about a week, not because it is so laborious, but because the printer probably has twenty other jobs going through at the same time. High Street instant-printers have become much more common in recent years. They will turn the job around quickly and cheaply, but the result might not be brilliant, due to the limitations of their machinery. If you get several quotes and see the respective samples of different printers you will soon see what level of quality you can afford.

If you have worked carefully, the sight of the finished job should cause you pleasure and a sense of relief. If all of the letters are blurred, or an inch has been chopped off the bottom, you can ask for a reprint or argue for a reduction in price.

The total job, at current prices might cost you about £70, made up as follows: Typesetting 100 words — £8.50; 4 PMTs — £14.00; Materials — £8.50; Instant Print 100 A3 posters — £16.50; Instant Print 500 A5 leaflets — £14.00; VAT — £9.25; Total — £70.75. These prices will soon be out of date, but I include them to show how to prepare a budget.

Evaluate the result

Finally, when the poster and leaflet have been distributed, watch the response. Get friends to ask questions for you. (Well, everyone will tell *you* that it is wonderful, won't they?) "Reviews" can help you refine your publicity skills, so take them seriously. If your posters get nicked you are probably doing well. Finally, note how many people come as a result of your effort, and work out a response rate for future reference.

This description of the publicity process may seem dry. There is a lot to remember and organize. But to use fully creative gifts in service of communicating, there must be a degree of professionalism in the finished product. Printing is not cheap, and having something printed from ill-prepared artwork is the most expensive of all.

Try it out... Publicity projects

Two projects for you to consider:

1. Your church has asked you to prepare local publicity to invite people in your community to their special Christmas service.

How would you interpret the worn-out Christmas images in a relevant way? What title would you give to the service? How would you use the Bible in your preparation, or in your publicity?

2. You have been asked to do a publicity poster promoting your church's series of Lent Bible study groups. Your target audience is the church members. The subject of the Lent groups is the Letter to the Philippians.

Look through Philippians. Read the whole book to start with, to get a feel for it.

Then think about:

1. What's the theme?
2. What are the most striking images?
3. How could you interpret these into an attractive poster?

A poster campaign

The advertising posters in Britain are reckoned by many to be the best in the world. They are strong, bright, and clever. They avoid "hard-sell" in favour of wit, novelty, and dynamic visual properties. Ironically, the quality and worth of the things being advertised is often not as good as the ads themselves. Why can't the same kind of style be used to focus attention on the really important issues of life?

If you enjoy puzzles, and have a good eye and ear for what makes people tick, the chances are that you can come up with ideas to present some aspect of the Christian faith through a poster. Posters for specific events have built-in limitations; they must include essential information, and they are only relevant for a short period of time leading up to the event. The posters we will consider here have a broader application. In a sense they are the event in themselves.

Advertising

Most people feel that they are above the ploys of adverts, that though ads are full of tricks and manipulative practices, it is only the naive who are influenced. Now a fair bit of the money spent on advertising is spent on research — finding out what the consumer thinks. It is only logical to assume that the people who are making ads know full-well that consumers feel immune. Yet the basic formula for advertising doesn't change, and large companies spend huge sums on more and more advertising. The inescapable conclusion is that although people may feel that ads don't influence them, it doesn't matter. The ads still work.

One of the reasons for the effectiveness of advertising imagery is that ads work a bit like mirrors. They hold up a picture of ourselves for our approval. They show hypothetical characters which are very compelling. They don't often say, "Buy this and become a charismatic, attractive, socialite", but rather, "Buy this because you already are a charismatic, attractive, socialite". We are prone to inflating our own self-image, so we fall for it, without even knowing what we are doing.

Images from the world of advertising become part of our common cultural perception. If we say that someone is "well-established", the mental pictures we have are heavily influenced by the images used in advertising to portray the "well-established". This circular, self-feeding process is tricky to interrupt, even for the purposes of analysis.

Ultimately all of the goods and services sold promise improvement of life-style, and imply improvement of the self. In one sense this can be viewed as a game in which the seller and buyer are both aware of the unwritten "rules" and exaggerations. Yet at another level the whole emphasis on "image" in advertising is a diversion from the discovery of our real identity in the design and plan of God. The subtle message in advertising telling us that we "already are the people we wish we were, we just need to show it", is almost right — except that material things are substituted for spiritual ones. In Christ we already are what we are meant to be — Christ's work is complete and total. We need to live it out. Seen in this light, the promises and puffery of advertising is a substitute for the truth. But we are willingly blinded.

Any attempt to critically examine advertising is an eye-opener. Why is that cooker photographed on a beach? What kind of environments usually feature in drinks ads? How is life assurance generally presented? How do ads use the theme of "security"? We are so accustomed to casual viewing of ads that it may even be hard to study them seriously and try to decode their messages. But if you do, such an exercise reveals that the values, logic of persuasion, and images used, are borrowed from our culture as a whole. The themes are the basic needs of men. The longing is for fulfilment and salvation. It is not that an elite corps of shady psychologists is forcing us to adopt new perspectives. Rather, ads are a reflection of us and show how insecure our pampered self-image really is. If you really wish to know what people in the West value, there can be no better place to look than at advertising, for beneath the polished surface there are some pretty dry bones.

Worked example... A poster

Posters usually have three components: headline, image, and byline. The first two function as "picture with caption" in most cases. The byline is either a conclusion, a qualification, or a hint about the real issue of the message. It is the most difficult bit to get right. Sometimes it is possible to create an image which can work without headline or byline.

For instance, imagine a poster to illustrate the first commandment. "Worship no god but me".

In the hype and adulation associated with the pop-music world this commandment is often broken (not that this is the only area!) An image of a typical rock-concert could be changed by placing a golden calf on stage in a spotlight and in front of a microphone. This image alone, although a bit cryptic, would be understood by those familiar with the Bible. The use of the verse as a headline would make the meaning quite explicit — perhaps too much so, as the image would become subordinate to the text and might lose power.

Take another example. When Jesus preaches to the crowds in Matthew 5–7 he makes many surprising statements. At the end, we

A POSTER ON THE THEME
'WORSHIP NO GOD BUT ME'
(SEE TEXT)

hear the listeners were "amazed at the way he taught". Why? Lets look at chapter 5 in which Jesus teaches the crowd of listeners the meaning of true happiness. None of the secular features of "happiness" figure. Instead Jesus talks about mourning, humility, mercy, and being persecuted.

As you read, make a note of the typical attitudes that Jesus was challenging. This radical reorientation is as much needed now as when Jesus spoke. Jesus used surprise throughout the "sermon": "You have heard it said . . . but now I tell you . . ." He is aware of how people think, and starting with common assumptions about morality, he proceeds to show the source of true righteousness in an attitude to God.

True Happiness

³"Happy are those who know they are spiritually poor; the Kingdom of heaven belongs to them!

⁴"Happy are those who mourn; God will comfort them!

⁵"Happy are those who are humble; they will receive what God has promised!

⁶"Happy are those whose greatest desire is to do what God requires; God will satisfy them fully!

⁷"Happy are those who are merciful to others; God will be merciful to them!

⁸"Happy are the pure in heart; they will see God!

⁹"Happy are those who work for peace; God will call them his children!

¹⁰"Happy are those who are persecuted because they do what God requires; the Kingdom of heaven belongs to them!

¹¹"Happy are you when people insult you and persecute you and tell all kinds of evil lies against you because you are my followers. ¹²Be happy and glad, for a great reward is kept for you in heaven. This is how the prophets who lived before you were persecuted.

(Matthew 5.3–12)

Rather than making a poster to illustrate a particular verse, we will try to make a visual/verbal combination which gets to the heart of Jesus' teaching on an issue. Here are the opening verses of chapter 6 — Jesus is at his most vivid as a teacher, on the subject of humility.

"Make certain you do not perform your religious duties in public so that people will see what you do. If you do these things publicly, you will not have any reward from your Father in heaven.
²"So when you give something to a needy person, do not make a big show of it, as the hypocrites do in the houses of worship and on the streets. They do it so that people will praise them. I assure you, they have already been paid in full. ³But when you help a needy person, do it in such a way that even your closest friend will not know about it. ⁴Then it will be a private matter. And your Father, who sees what you do in private, will reward you.

⁵"When you pray, do not be like the hypocrites! They love to stand up and pray in the houses of worship and on the street corners, so that everyone will see them. I assure you, they have already been paid in full. ⁶But when you pray, go to your room, close the door,

and pray to your Father, who is unseen. And your Father who sees what you do in private, will reward you.

[7]"When you pray, do not use a lot of meaningless words, as the pagans do, who think that their gods will hear them because their prayers are long. [8]Do not be like them. Your Father already knows what you need before you ask him.

(Matthew 6.1–8)

As you read, what visual images come to mind?

Make your own list of images before going on to look at the rest of this example.

Jesus is attacking pride. It is an echo of the humility theme of chapter 5. What can be said about humility through calling attention to pride? Bragging, self-satisfaction, insensitivity, devious dealings — there are a host of practices associated with pride.

Following this line of thought, the phrase "puffed up" comes to mind. "Inflated" . . . perhaps a figure with a hose going from his mouth to his own ear, swelling his own head . . . or maybe a figure with a speech bubble full of overbearing, self-serving phrases . . .

The exercise of discovering an idea is exciting. As you begin to formulate ideas you may start with an image which will suggest a new copy-line, which will prompt a new image. As your associative process generates these ideas, jot them down and keep going. Go back to the passage again and again to recharge your imagination.

Technical tips... Printing posters

If you have a major event to advertise, such as described earlier in the chapter, you will probably want to have your posters printed professionally. However, if you are experimenting and testing ideas for response, commercial printing is out of the question.

■ The photocopier can come to the rescue. If your type and image are clear and strong the photocopies will give a dense black image (you may have to hunt a bit for the best machine). Sizes larger than A3 can be made up by cutting photocopies together. You can add colour to the photocopy using a water-based marker. Spirit-based markers will dissolve the image — they can be used for artistic ends, but will muddy the ends of your felt-tipped pens.

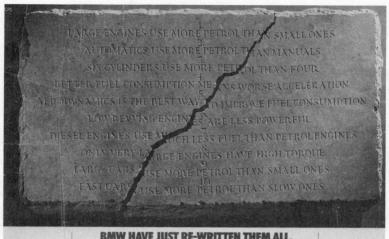

BMW HAVE JUST RE-WRITTEN THEM ALL.

Above, the conventional wisdom of the car industry. A set of rules that can be summed up in one word: compromise.

Below, a car that owes little to convention and nothing to compromise.

order to shrink fuel consumption you have to shrink the engine.

The eta is a smooth running, 2.7 litre, six cylinder engine. Yet it uses less fuel engines of just 1.6 litres and four

Two adverts which use popular images of the Ten Commandments and the Garden of Eden to advertise cars and The Times. *What do you think of them? What image of the Bible do you think they reflect?*

■ Other means for introducing colour should also be considered: spray paint (with or without stencils); simple linoleum blocks; chalk-dust rubbed with cotton wool, etc. A black and white poster with a spot of bright colour can be more visible than some full-colour posters.

■ There is a slightly more complex process which is worth knowing about: screen-printing. In this process ink is squeezed through a mesh-supported stencil on to the paper. At the low-tech end of the process, it is possible to produce good results with about £20 worth of materials. With a bigger outlay you can use photo-sensitive films and print text as fine as that on this page — and do it on the kitchen table. If you are intrigued by this, find several books on the process. Several, because some are written for the large-scale commercial screen-printer, and others are rather simplistic. Best of all, get a few people together (including an art student?) to help set up a DIY screen-printing frame.

 Displaying posters

Think about the location carefully.

■ Is it visible?

■ Will your precious creation have to compete with the usual ads for free kittens, roofing experts, and yoga classes?

■ How long do people spend in the area?

■ Are they normally preoccupied with other things?

■ Are they in the company of other people?

■ Do you need permission to put a poster up?

■ If a poster is placed where queues form, you can have longer copy or an intricate image which will hold someone's attention. A poster placed in a recreation area shouldn't be too intellectual . . .

There are no rules, but it pays to consider the environment and the potential viewer's likely frame of mind. Don't think of your audience as some vague, vast public. Aim, instead, at the people you know.

You will probably want to make a number of copies. You will want to keep a copy for yourself and to have a spare ready in the event that the one you put up is defaced or stolen. If you have a good site, a series of posters could develop a theme. A well-thought out and nicely designed poster is up for a week, and is noticed. If it is followed by another, equally good, interest will increase. By the time a third poster follows, people will start talking about them.

Try it out... **A poster**

Work up a poster that explores, explains, or challenges:

■ Ideas people have about being "good"

■ Beliefs, misunderstandings, and hopes about after-life

■ Religious words which are often misunderstood — salvation, hell, sin, forgiveness, etc.

WHAT COPY WOULD YOU WRITE TO MAKE THIS BRAVE APPROACH WORK?

89

■ Notions about human progress and the source of human ability

■ Any one of the Ten Comandments — or a series of ten posters covering all of them

■ Current events from God's perspective

■ The Bible — particularly a poster which encourages people to read it

Conclusion

The key to a successful poster often lies in the ability to see your faith as a non-believer sees it. One Christian group put up a poster with a headline in bold type saying, "Christians are dogmatic, unrealistic, hypocritical, and naive". The byline said simply, "See for yourself. Room 212 at 1.30p.m." This is intriguing, due to the unexpected "confession" which paradoxically challenges the very thing it states.

The energy and cost of pursuing the poster-medium may deter you, but if the projects are tackled with a group to share the load, the stress can almost vanish. The next time you are reading the Bible and a verse comes home to you with unusual force . . . think about how a poster might be used to express it.

6. Art in the church family

The exercises in this chapter are intended to help you draw others into using their creative abilities to explore the Bible. Some of them are applicable to children's work or to youth groups. Others have a less specific application and can be used wherever you see fit. Activities which involve handwork are excellent for helping people to get to know one another. The products of such exercises can become objects for discussion. The atmosphere in a room with ten or so people busy making things is very comfortable.

There is real satisfaction to be had in working with our hands. The dynamics of the process are curious. When we start working on something, we often have a clear picture of what it is we are about to make. As we set to work, we soon encounter the recalcitrance of material, the inadequacy of tools, and the limits of our skill. Sometimes the combination of these is enough to cause us to abandon the project. It is very unusual to complete a work of art or craft without altering the design in the process. Every step of the way seems to throw up problems, and it is solving these problems that provides the sense of accomplishment. We discover effects that were not expected. The progress of a project becomes a dialogue between us and the materials we use.

The value of handwork has long been recognized by those who advise the physically or emotionally handicapped. Handwork is a crucial component of any programme for children. What a shame that it is not used more for the rest of us! Many people have hobbies that involve handwork, to be sure, but by-and-large people feel that they haven't time, talent, or opportunity. One of the great disruptions of modern life is that most of us do not have the chance to see a project through from start to finish. Instead what we do at the office, shop, or factory, is only one stage in a larger process we do not control.

Starting an art group

One way to make use of the exercise outlined here would be to set up a small "art" group. Give it a name, — Picassos Anonymous, The

Close Brush Club — and invite those whom you think would enjoy it. If you have the room to meet in a home, so much the better. The group could meet fortnightly. How about providing a very simple meal — bread and cheese? You don't want it to take too much time. A light meal will help make people comfortable, and it will be possible to start on the evening's activity while late-comers are still eating. To start, you might want to play a few drawing games. The evening could then move on to a specific project such as those mentioned in previous chapters, or to individual projects. There aren't enough different suggestions here to keep a group active for ever, so you'll have to come up with your own ideas. Of course, you may discover that there is no need to have something new prepared for each session. People are usually happy to continue a project over quite a few sessions. If you do plan to do some of the messier projects, be sure to get help with cleaning up afterwards!

Such a group can also be a way to introduce non-Christians to Christians. If you think it appropriate, mention to prospective non-Christian participants that the group is "a number of Christians who get together to do art". Social encounters of this informal nature will not cause undue pressure, and conversation will naturally touch on the Christian faith without seeming like "a set up". You may be surprised to discover the interest that non-Christians will show in working from Bible themes.

If you discover an activity which is a great success, do it again in another context. It helps if others in the group have told their friends about the "great time" they had marbling paper, or whatever. For instance, if you have devised some simple means for printing, an evening in November devoted to making Christmas cards is likely to be very popular.

Many art and craft activities do not require tight scheduling and dynamic leadership. The very character of creative work seems to generate a relaxed easy-going style. However, unless there is some structure, people may lose interest and eventually cease to come. Remember that responsiveness to the needs and wishes of the group is essential. A few tips:

■ Don't demonstrate anything that you haven't already figured out. Practice several times beforehand. Be sure that everything you need is at hand. Don't fumble apologetically; answer questions briefly.

92

■ Be realistic about what can be accomplished in the allotted time, and don't take the whole time with a demonstration.

■ Remember that you are trying to encourage others. They may be extremely hesitant about the enterprise. Be helpful without being domineering, praise what is good and be gentle in giving advice.

■ If all of the materials are to be provided, pay for the first session out of your pocket and at the beginning of a second session ask for a contribution from each participant to cover costs. You may want to delegate this to someone else. Investigate cheap sources of materials. There are a number of suppliers to schools which can be talked into supplying limited quantities. Printers will often sell off-cuts of paper for next-to-nothing.

■ Try to find others who can lead an evening. There may be someone with experience of book-binding, for instance, who could be brought along after the group has learned how to marble paper. If you are able to link events together in a logical sequence, so much the better, but don't force your programme on reluctant participants.

■ Background music can help create a feeling of ease. Avoid extreme forms.

■ Make a point of getting to know everyone in the group. For the first few meetings it is a good idea to ring everyone before the meeting and remind them about the meeting and anything they should bring along.

■ Try to bring along samples, books, or anything which relates to the activity, or which is visually exciting. Encourage others to do the same. This can be helpful if someone is stuck for an idea. The more interaction you can encourage among members, the better.

Projects for art groups

Most of the activities listed here are quite easy to do. The cost of material for most is low. They are arranged from the simplest to the more complex. Of course, many of the other projects suggested in this book can be tried out in your art group. Some of the activities require preparation or collection of material. Don't leave this to the last minute. You will notice that some of these activities are ideal for the treatment of Bible themes, and that others are less so. Similarly, some are appropriate for children, and others aren't.

Try it out... Marbling paper

The rich, swirling patterns of marbled paper are now back in fashion. Book covers, lamp shades, song books, and many other things are enhanced by marbling.

The most sophisticated technique uses exotic materials like Irish seaweed, alum water, and ox gall. A more practical method is as follows:

■ Mix a little wall paper paste or glue-size into some cold water. The mixture should be thinner than for wall-papering. This is then poured into a large shallow pan — a big photographic tray is ideal.

■ Ordinary artist's oil colour is thinned with white spirit or turps substitute, and put in large-mouthed glass jars.

■ The colour is dropped lightly on to the surface of the size. A drop of colour should spread to form a circle of about two or three inches in diameter. Add colour until the whole of the surface is covered.

■ This surface can then be swirled with a needle or a "comb" made by evenly-spaced pins protruding from a card.

■ When you are rapturously excited by the design, carefully drop a sheet of thin paper onto the surface. Wait a moment and then lift the sheet off by one corner. Some of the paste will have stuck to the

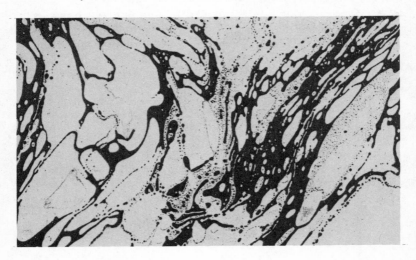

paper as well as the pattern. The excess paste can be washed off straight away without damaging the pattern.

■ Finished, dry papers can be glued to small card boxes, metal tins, book covers, even Bibles. With a bit of practice it is possible to marble the edges of book pages by clamping the pages between two pieces of stiff card of the same dimension as the pages. Practice this on a discarded book before attempting it on your Bible!

Try it out... Collage

This process is so well known as to need little explanation. Basically you glue bits of paper to a sheet of card.

If you plan to include objects and make an "assemblage", ensure that the support is strong enough to hold everything together.

Thin coloured tissue-paper works very well for collage as it is translucent and the intensity of colour can be built up by increasing the number of layers. For such thin absorbent papers it is best to apply the glue to the top of the paper and let it soak through — attempts to lift tissue-paper covered with glue are very amusing. Put the tissue paper where you want it, and gently brush slightly thinned PVA glue on top.

A variation of the collage techniques uses imprints from printed photos. A colour photo from a magazine is moistened with white spirit or turps substitute. In a few seconds the thinner will begin to soften the printing ink. A piece of paper can be placed over the image, and a pale version of the image can be transferred by rubbing the back of the paper with the bowl of a table spoon. (Incidentally photocopies can also be transferred by this technique, or by first spraying the photocopy with fixative and transferring the image before the fixative dries.) The soft images produced by this "trick" combine well with patches of colour made with tissue paper.

As collage is a rather messy affair, it is advisable to have a disciplined approach. Try arrangements of the elements dry before pasting everything together and then changing your mind.

If the base material is a thin, translucent sheet such as rice paper, collage can be used to hang in front of windows. This can be an economical and effective way to decorate a sanctuary or church hall.

You will add an extra dimension to your project if your collages are on a selected Bible theme or passage. Get one of the group to choose a couple of passages that bear upon a theme, possibly from the short-list below, or from the general list of themes on pages 9–11.

Symbols associated with God

- the fountain
- Manna
- light
- tree
- tower

- fire
- mountain
- foundation
- the rock

 Greeting cards

The giant greeting card industry is supported by our appetite for novel ways to remember things. Everyone likes cards, but many of the cards designed to celebrate Christian festivals no longer have any Christian content. How would you design an Easter or Christmas card?

Making cards is an exciting group activity. Start by obtaining some stiff paper from a printer. For a pound or two the printer will trim these scraps to the sizes you want. Try to get an assortment of different colours, textures, and thicknesses. Postcard size (A6) and A5 are good sizes. The latter can be folded to allow for text on the inside. Some photocopiers can handle a sheet as small as A6 if the paper isn't too heavy. Use some of the printing techniques described below to manufacture your cards.

An appropriate way to introduce some Bible study into the process of creating a Christmas card:

■ Choose three Bible passages which in various ways are always associated with Christmas — for example Isaiah 61.1–4; Luke 2.8–20; John 1.1–9. Then choose three possible audiences for the Christmas cards — for example: 1. A card for you to send to your non-Christian friends; 2. A card for W. H. Smith or a card shop to sell to the general public; 3. A card for you to send to Christian friends.

■ Each person must take one passage, and one "audience" (there are nine possible combinations) and prepare a card, with a design, and a message (set a word limit — seven words?) that express the truth of that passage in a way suited to that audience.

You can also have fun making up special "days", and cards to go with it. For example, a Bible study on Wealth and Poverty can be followed by a task to create a card for newly announced "National Wealth Day" — cards which are supposed to help the recipient think about the Bible's teaching on wealth and poverty!

You might want to make up a collection of the cards as gifts to the elderly or infirm.

Technical tips... **Low-tec printing**

Potato-prints, lino-cuts, and wood-blocks are familiar techniques capable of making quite a good impression. The potato does have its limits, though, and can't be relied on to reproduce fine detail or print the whole image every time. Block-printing is better.

■ If you can get hold of an old mangle, it can easily be converted into a block printing-press (see illustration overleaf). Get a small sheet of plywood to fit through the rollers and cut a square of an old blanket to the same size.

Roll a dab of ink out on a sheet of glass with a hard rubber roller and then ink the block.

Put the block face-up on the ply, then the paper, followed by the blanket. Crank this sandwich through the press, having first adjusted the distance between the rollers.

■ Try printing from "found" objects — weathered wood, old shoes, crumpled cloth, or whatever will fit through the press in place of the wood block. The results will be unpredictable, but you are likely to have a few real winners. If you do, it can always be reproduced on a photocopier.

■ Shapes cut from card can be glued to a block of wood and printed, too.

■ If you can lay your hands on some old PVC glazing plastic, or Perspex, this can be used to make simple "etchings". Place the clear sheet over a drawing you have made, and trace off the design by scratching the surface of the plastic with a needle.

Wipe a dab of ink on to the surface and rub it well into the scratches. It won't take much ink.

Rub a little talcum powder onto the heel of your hand and wipe the surface of the plastic to remove excess ink. The object is to leave ink in the cracks but not on the unscratched areas.

the poorman's etching press

The Mangle

ADJUST THE
PRESSURE ON
THE TOP ROLLER
FOR THE THICKNESS
OF THE PRINTING
BLOCK OR PLATE

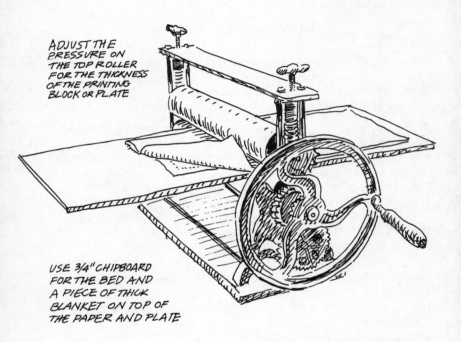

USE 3/4" CHIPBOARD
FOR THE BED AND
A PIECE OF THICK
BLANKET ON TOP OF
THE PAPER AND PLATE

IF YOU ARE BUYING A MANGLE FROM A JUNK SHOP
LOOK AT THE TEETH ON THE DRIVE GEARS. WORN
TEETH ARE OKAY BUT BROKEN GEAR WHEEL CAN
CAUSE PROBLEMS. IF THE TOP ROLLER IS BADLY
WORN (IT PROBABLY WILL BE) YOU CAN GREATLY
IMPROVE THE PRINTING PERFORMANCE IF YOU
TAKE THE TOP ROLLER OUT AND HAVE IT TRUED
ON A LATHE. A MACHINE SHOP SHOULD DO IT FOR
A FEW POUNDS.

Soak some thick paper in a tray of water for about ten minutes, then blot out the excess moisture before draping it on the plastic.

Print it as for block-prints. (The paper must be moist to be forced into the scratches and pick up the ink.)

Other textures can be achieved by gently rubbing areas of the surface with nail polish remover or any other chemical which attacks the plastic. This will produce a pleasant "grainy" effect.

■ Stencil techniques are also useful for multiple-copies. Masks cut from card can be spattered with a paint-charged toothbrush, or sprayed with aerosol paint. Patterns made by folding and cutting paper can be combined with other stencils to make very interesting forms.

■ Foam paint-rollers can be engraved to make simple decorative patterns. Resultant prints can be embellished by hand or overprinted by other methods.

Try it out... **Making puppets**

Puppets fascinate everyone. A good puppeteer will hold a crowd with the most implausible selection of characters. The real art, as they say, is in the telling, but it helps to have good puppets.

The simplest puppets are no more than a cardboard face on a stick. We looked quickly at those on page 35. Add a cloth gown and a hand attached to another stick, and this basic creature becomes animate.

Glove-puppets require a bit more work. The standard toilet-roll-tube-in-the-head arrangement is quite workable if not the most comfortable device to wear. Commercial papier-mache materials are excellent for modelling heads, and have the advantage of being very light.

Air-curing spray-foams are available from hobby shops and builder's merchants, which can be sculpted after they have hardened. Spray some on a loose-fitting glove, wiggle your fingers for a few moments as it starts to cure and, presto, you have the base for a custom-fitted puppet.

More sophisticated versions can be carved out of soft woods (balsa, lime, and jelotong are particularly suitable), and painted.

Features can afford to be rather coarse — big eyes, ears, nose, and

A SIMPLE STICK PUPPET

PAINTED
CARDBOARD
HEAD AND
HANDS

CLOTH
BODY

THIN
BLACK
CONTROL
RODS

WORKS BEST AGAINST
A BLACK BACKDROP

lips will be seen better than delicate ones. A long gown, reaching nearly to the elbow, gives the figure more presence.

Velcro on the hands makes it possible for figures to "hold" objects. These props also need to be designed.

Key characters can be equipped with moving jaws, either in the fashion of a sock-puppet, or with a proper articulated joint. Look at some of the books on puppets to see what tricks have been used to make one hand behave like a whole creature.

This activity will invariably instigate quite a lot of spontaneous role play. Nourish these seeds, and try to put a few scenes together. Encourage participants to develop consistent "personalities" for their characters. A buffoon who always misunderstands can be an asset when it comes to communicating with children, as they will delight in correcting him.

There is great scope here for treating characters from the Bible. By all means get everyone involved in the acting and story development, too. Start by acting out some of the parables, for example "The Friend at Midnight" as related in Luke 11.1–10.

Try it out... Making books

A hand-made book is a special possession. The book-binder's art is in a period of revival at the moment. Limited edition volumes with tooled leather covers and traditional sewn spines fetch prices which reflect the time put into their manufacture. You may know someone who does book-binding. If so, ask them to explain, or lead a group session. The methods described here are short-cuts. Use the books for sketching, or for collections of drawings, or as note books. Notes of what you learn from Bible study can take on a special meaning if preserved in a book you have made yourself.

There is a commercial process called "perfect binding" in which cut sheets of paper are edge-glued, like a scrap-pad. Until recently this process qualified for the most ill-named of all time. We've all had paperbacks that fell apart. Modern glues are better.

A very simple way to make such a book is as follows: clamp the stack of pages, with two slightly heavier sheets for covers, between two sheets of thick plywood, so that the paper just protrudes beyond the ply on the spine.

With a very fine saw, notch the spine with thin grooves across the spine. Apply a coat of white wood-working glue, and while the glue is still wet, lay a strip of linen "scrim" or any thin, open weave cloth, into the glue. The cloth will make the spine tougher. Leave the pages cramped overnight.

When dry, remove the book and put a strip of adhesive-backed cloth-tape over the spine, pressing it firmly onto the dried glue.

Simple "perfect bound" books are good for children's events. You could prepare each cover with the name of the child, and suggest themes. It is even better to prepare the covers separately and make up the book after the child has produced a number of drawings and some text. You can then help them make their own drawings into books, a real thrill.

There are many video recorders around, but less video cameras. If you have access to one, and are among a group that enjoys acting, there is no reason why you shouldn't experiment with this exciting medium. Videos can be hired at a reasonable weekly rate. To be sure, video requires a lot of effort, and a camera and recorder alone won't produce slick, broadcast quality programmes. You won't be able to edit without either paying quite a lot of money, or "knowing someone" with the right gear. But even with a camera and recorder only, you can start to come to terms with the potential of moving images. It has the added perk that you can see the results of your filming immediately.

The effects of camera angles, length of shot, lighting, framing, and so-forth are better left to a specialist book on the subject, but unless you start to experiment, the books won't be much help. Handling the camera and learning to "think" through the lens will take time.

A rather enjoyable way to begin is to give the camera to each person (or to a pair) for an hour, and ask them to shoot no more than two minutes. For each person's turn as cameraman, someone else serves as assistant to help juggle the equipment, position actors, etc. The camera person/director may be allowed a limited number of actors, or whatever other constraints you decide as a group. These initial projects will help to get people thinking about story-lines, the continuity of movement and technical effects.

The same exercise can be extended for five-minute films, and so on. It is important to start small and to set limits because film is a very disciplined medium. It requires great imagination, yes, but it also demands a grasp of "rules".

For each person's project, choose a biblical theme. Some examples are given in the list below. Each one has been summarized by a catch-phrase. Look through the Bible passages suggested, and others that come to mind. Each person must use their two minutes to shoot a sequence that summarizes the theme. It could be a symbolic treatment; a dance; a sketch; a story; or a combination of all four.

■ God chooses the weak (Moses — Exodus 6.28—7.7; Gideon — Judges 6.1–40; Mary — Luke 1.46–56)

■ It was lost but now it's found (Luke 15; Isaiah 53.6)

■ The foolish (particularly as described in Proverbs; Matthew 7.24 – 27; Matthew 25.1–13)

■ Richman, poorman (much of Proverbs again; Mark 10.17–31; 12.41–44)

Simpler still, select up to ten amusing proverbs — write each on a separate slip of paper. Shuffle them, and get each person (or pair) to pick one. They must use their two minutes to present their interpretation of that proverb.

Try it out... **An animated film**

A more expensive option, but one with greater flexibility, is a Super 8 movie. Three minutes shoot by rapidly when filming summer water-fights with the family in the garden, but can go a long way if you make an animated film. Again, you are advised to consult books on this fascinating subject for detailed guidance. There are some simple techniques, though, which can make film-making well within the reach of a small group. Don't start a film project unless you are fairly sure that your group has the patience to see it through.

Because you won't have the facilities to make a technically flawless production, it is better not even to try. If the motion is a bit jerky, and miscellaneous shadows appear, don't worry. Concentrate instead on a good story. Start with a few ten-or-fifteen-second films.

■ You will need a Super 8 camera with a fitting for a cable release. This allows you to click-off each frame as a separate picture.

■ You will also need a consistent light source. An electronic flash-unit works well, particularly if the light is "bounced" off a large white card onto the subject.

Here are three different ways of creating an animated film:

Using Plasticine

With the camera set up on a tripod, and focused on a table top, you can manipulate a ball of plasticine to make it undergo remarkable transformations.

Develop a rhythm of slightly shaping the clay, clicking the shutter and shaping the clay further . . . A ball becomes an egg, the egg wiggles and cracks open, a chick-head pops out, which grows into a hen, which lays an egg . . .

This technique is so much fun that you may want to stick with it. It is a very good exercise to develop a feeling for the right speed of animation.

Using flat-puppets

Another technique depends on the use of flat-puppets with movable joints. A light coating of spray-adhesive on the back will keep the puppet in place on the background while it is photographed, and will allow you to reposition the movable elements. Long backdrops painted on lining paper can be moved underneath a figure to give the impression of walking (when combined with the movement of the legs, of course).

Whatever subject you choose, everyone can help in the planning stages, and various tasks can be assigned to members of the group. One person prepares backgrounds as sketches, and others help colour them in; someone makes the basic puppets, and someone else makes puppets for unusual positions. When it comes to shooting, one person can operate the camera, another the background, and another the puppets. A fourth person is needed to monitor timings and keep track of the script. Be sure to shoot a bit of test-footage before proceeding to the finished film. Tricky sequences are best shot twice, to allow for editing.

Using people

Hilarous films can be made by animating people. With the camera on the tripod, position the actor and instruct him to move his feet two-feet-forward on your command. Take a frame, and have the actor move again. Take another frame, and so on. In the finished film the actor will appear to zoom around at breakneck speed without ever moving his feet. This technique can be applied to almost any action. It's great fun, but can be used to serious effect. You could produce an effective parody of the modern rat-race, and contrast it with passages from the Bible about the true purpose of life.

This brief description of the process cannot convey the excitement of the whole process. It is hard work, but worth it. Seeing the finished footage will be a mixture of delight and agony. In the context of a group, a "feel" for the medium will quickly develop, and you will acquire a better idea of what is feasible. Although film is unlikely to be the first group art exercise you will choose, it does provide enormous potential for expression.

Projects for youth groups

Most of the material in this book can be used with youth groups. Projects such as video, animated films, murals, and exercises such as the drawing games are ideal.

But there is a special consideration when working with teenagers. There is a stage during adolescence when artistic activity is a no-go area. Anything that involves drawing or painting is considered childish. On the other hand, there are a number of techniques of visual expression which are uniquely suited to teenagers.

Try it out... **Graffiti**

You don't need reminding that this is a favourite "art-form". One minute in a bus shelter or a station will suffice. Most public graffiti is fairly distasteful.

In the church, however, some people have rescued graffiti and used it to help express Christian ideas. They have designated one wall in the youth-club room a graffiti wall. Either they have covered it with rolls of lining paper, or have chosen a wall that is not precious! Anything that members of the youth group want to "express" publicly can be painted, drawn, scrawled, or splashed on this official graffiti wall.

When the wall is out of date you simply remove the lining paper, or paint over the wall with a cheap emulsion, and then start again.

You might want to get some rules as to what can/cannot be put on the graffiti wall.

When doing Bibles studies, for example the teachings of Jesus in the parables, the graffiti wall can come in useful. Split into small groups. Each small group studies the same parable and comes up with a slogan that expresses its message. Each group then puts their slogan on the graffiti wall.

So what was learnt from Bible study is there on the wall as a constant reminder for the next few weeks and months.

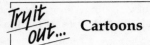

Cartoons

Some groups might contain a gifted cartoonist. Teenagers particularly seem to enjoy caricatures.

Get a member of your church who is able to draw good cartoons to come and lead a session. Using illustrations of famous cartoonists, anything from Mr Men through to Giles, he/she can show how a cartoon works, and how to use exaggerated features to give character to your drawings. Then get the groups to try out their own skills.

The wittiest cartoons can be used in the church magazine. It can become a regular feature — one way for the youth group to participate in the church.

Tee-shirts

An official group tee-shirt always goes down well, and it is quite easy to get them made. Tee-shirt printers can be found in yellow pages. If you order at least a dozen tee-shirts you can get them printed quite reasonably, from whatever artwork you provide. If you have experimented with screenprinting, you probably will have discovered the thrill of printing your own.

You can run a fascinating session to design a group tee-shirt. Your tee-shirt will probably need to contain two components:

1. Group name — After Eights, The Rockers, The Fish Shop, etc.
2. Some symbol of what the group stands for — a Bible, a cross, a fish, a question mark, a dove, etc.

A tee-shirt session should begin with a discussion of what the group is about. Then go on to "brain-storm" possible symbols for the tee-shirt.

Then, in pairs or individually, design your own picture.

At the end of the session the group should pick one or two designs which should be passed over to the best artist, or someone else from the church who is able to prepare artwork from it, for the tee-shirt printer.

Projects for children

Here are suggestions for Bible-related activities, some of which could be continued over a few consecutive weeks. As most are based on model-making, be sure to have a good stock of material to hand. See Technical tips . . ., page 109.

For older groups, the model-making itself can have a serious educational aim and involve children in researching Bible background.

Try it out... ## An ark

A model of the ark, and animals. The actual shape of the ark is conjecture, but it was big.

If you have the space, make a ten-foot long ark from cardboard packing boxes, with animals and all components made to scale. The description of the ark is to be found in Genesis 6.9–22. Make a door in the side, big enough to allow children to "enter" the ark, and put the animals in "cages", made by attaching small boxes to the inside of the ark walls — see the illustration.

A CARDBOARD ARK

LARGE CARDBOARD BOXES ARE OFTEN AVAILABLE FROM APPLIANCE DEALERS. FOR THIS ARK YOU WILL NEED AT LEAST SIX.

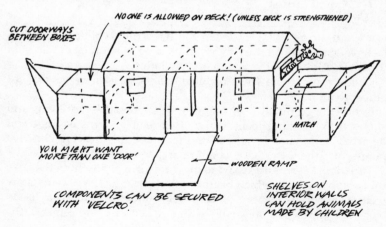

NO ONE IS ALLOWED ON DECK! (UNLESS DECK IS STRENGTHENED)

CUT DOORWAYS BETWEEN BOXES

YOU MIGHT WANT MORE THAN ONE 'DOOR'

HATCH

WOODEN RAMP

COMPONENTS CAN BE SECURED WITH 'VELCRO'

SHELVES ON INTERIOR WALLS CAN HOLD ANIMALS MADE BY CHILDREN

The ark and animals should be painted by the children. As a spin off, you may want to trace some references to animals in the Bible.

Try it out... Maps

Children like maps, particularly if they have a hand in creating them. There are many stories in the Bible which are better visualized with maps.

The story of the Exodus can be made as a combination of a map and an Advent calendar. Flaps on the surface of the map have Bible references on them, and when the flap is lifted it reveals a picture of the scene.

A relief-map of lands where Bible events were played out can be made from reference books. Exaggerate the relief, using expanded polystyrene or papier mache. It will help children understand that the Bible lands are real places, and help lead to confidence in the Bible's account.

This can be turned into a game. Place names mentioned in the Bible appear in a particular colour. Players aim to "visit" as many places in their team colours as possible! But they can only move to a place when they can tell what happened there.

Try it out... Games

Games are already widely used in youth work and children's work as ice-breakers. Here's a way they can be used to stimulate interest in the Bible. It's a visual variation on "charades".

Children make drawings of Bible events, places, or people, for others to identify.

Divide the group into two teams. One team makes a drawing and shows it to the other team. If the other team recognizes the event depicted in the drawing the team that made the drawing gets two points, and the team that recognizes it gets one point.

Variations: Teams are asked to draw pictures of anything they can think of in the Bible which begins with a certain letter. Teams draw pictures of objects mentioned in the Bible, and the other team has to work out somewhere in the Bible that this occurs. For example, the letter chosen is "S". One team draws a picture of a sheep, and the other team suggest it can be found in the Parable of the lost sheep. This type of game will encourage good familiarity with the Bible.

Try it out... A model of the sacred tent (or tabernacle)

The elaborate description of the sacred tent (or "tabernacle") in the book of Exodus shows us that God valued craftsmanship and order. The building was very practical, beautiful, and above all symbolic. In making a model of it there is not only the chance to see how the original was arranged, but also the opportunity to understand those complex ceremonial laws which found their focus in the sacred tent. This activity could help adults. It could help you read the book of Leviticus with new interest.

The model can be of any scale you wish, but if it is more than two-feet long, there will be more scope for detail. There are a number of books with "artists" reconstructions of the tabernacle, (for example *The Good News Bible Colour Reference Edition*, page 173) and you will want your group to consult a few of them. As soon as the scale is established each component can be made by a different small group.

Technical tips... Model-making supplies

In model-making a little organization can mean the difference between chaos and success. This is especially true when working with children. It is worth having a stock of materials kept under lock-and-key. Tools like scalpels are essential, but highly dangerous. Don't leave them lying around. Some useful tools and materials are:

■ An A3-size cutting mat. You can use a piece of heavy card, but scalpels and craft knives will make short work of it. A proper "Olfa" cutting-mat is rather expensive, but lasts for years.

■ A scalpel. The standard "Swann and Morton" type is probably best. You can hone the blade on a pocket-stone if you are loathe to change blades often. Keep it sharp. A sharp knife is far less dangerous than a blunt one. Use a "Stanley knife" for heavy work.

■ A heavy-metal straight-edge. Used in conjunction with the cutting-mat. The rubber-backed, non-slip ones are good.

■ A can of spray adhesive. The sort made for display work is very sticky, but strong. Other useful adhesives: white woodworker's glue, a Pritt stick, UHU, and double-sided tape.

■ A spray-box. Make your own by cutting the top off a cardboard box so that the walls are about ten inches deep. Stretch masking tape across the top at about three inch intervals. Put the item you want to coat with adhesive on the tape-strips, and spray so that the overspray goes into the box.

■ A "knife-saw". This is a very fine craft-saw which will cut small sections of metal, plastic, or wood.

■ Adhesive backed Velcro, which comes as two parts, the "hooks" and the "loops". Velcro is fantastically useful. Large cardboard constructions can be jointed together so as to enable them to be dismantled. A strip of "hooks" on the wall can hold light tools stuck with "loops", etc. The model of the tabernacle described in the text could use Velcro to allow the model to be neatly packed up. The non-adhesive variety will join banners together to make a larger one, or will attach banners to the wall.

■ Styrofoam or polystyrene. The light, white foam blocks used to pack household electrical goods and hi-fi. This can be cut with a sharp saw or knife. An even better way is to make a "hot-wire cutter". A fine metal guitar string is stretched across a wooden bow, and the ends can be wired to a twelve-volt car battery. The wire will get quite hot, and will cut through the polystyrene like butter. The wire can also be fixed with a jigsaw-like arm to a plywood table, to facilitate cutting slabs or strips. The foam can be painted with water-based paints, although it is difficult to get a smooth finish.

■ Ripstop nylon. The stuff used for making parachutes and kites. Very thin and strong. It can be used to make translucent banners (or kites), and has many uses in strengthening cardboard models and constructions.

■ Clamps. Make simple ones by gluing strips of wood to clothes pegs (the type with metal coil springs). These are invaluable for holding lightweight bits together while glue sets.

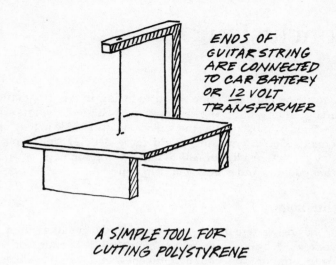

ENDS OF
GUITAR STRING
ARE CONNECTED
TO CAR BATTERY
OR 12 VOLT
TRANSFORMER

A SIMPLE TOOL FOR
CUTTING POLYSTYRENE

■ Wood. Particularly useful types are white pine, balsa, jelutong, and lime. The last two sorts carve very well. Jelutong is a wonderful material to work with.

■ Tweezers for little bits!

Conclusion

What can you hope to achieve by introducing an arts programme in your church or group? The entertainment value of the arts will be appreciated by most people, but will you really be able to help others experience God's word and world more deeply? You should be looking for that result, but realize that it won't happen overnight.

What qualities and events will help you?

Enthusiasm

Don't be disheartened if it is your enthusiasm rather than your artwork which has the most effect. Your attitude to your work, your desire to communicate, your inventiveness and warmth — these are the things which will make others take note. There is nothing sacred about the arts, at least no more than any other area of life. Introducing visual elements into the life of a church is unlikely to transform the congregation. Some people will praise your efforts, others will appear to ignore them. If your campaign for the arts is too strident, you may even alienate some members. If you fish for compliments you will only contribute to a common opinion about artists. Strive for humility.

Workshops

Workshops are the best way to spread enthusiasm. Look for opportunities to involve others. Consider inviting a group of people around for a meal with the intention of talking to them about the arts. When you invite them say something like: "We would like to make an artistic contribution to the life of the church, but we really need to know what people want. Can you come along and tell us what you think of arts in the context of the church?" If there is a skeptical or a particularly stern element in the church this is a surefire manner of disarming them. It is not only a ploy, though, for dialogue will benefit you. You will interest people in the arts if they see your interest coupled to a real interest in them.

An "arts day" or "crafts day" might help you spread interest — particularly if there is a core-group of keen artists in your church.

This is more formal than a workshop, combining speakers with artistic activity. A possible outlines is in the Appendix, on page 115.

Service

The artist is in a good position to be a servant. He can present tasty things, work hard but unobtrusively to make an environment pleasant, and be true and faithful. This, of course, is the model for all Christians. The gift of art is to be shared, like all of God's gifts. There are times when you will be at a loss as to what to do, and times when you doubt if the arts are of value. Although this is perfectly natural, it is helpful to remember that the unique constellation of gifts we have from God lose value if they are spent simply trying to please ourselves.

Communication

Many of the negative comments about "modern" art arise from the artist's inability or unwillingness to communicate about his activity at a level which can be understood. Don't fall into the trap of using obscure artistic lingo. The effort made to communicate about your art will also help to clarify your own thinking. It is just as when you hear a story and then tell it to someone else. The act of telling fixes the content in your memory.

To take an even more pertinent example, our faith becomes real to us in proportion to our expression of it. We can pride ourselves on the depth of our knowledge of the Bible, but if we never talk about it, never attempt to express it in our own words, we will not experience the "abundant life" we claim to know. In our day and age the notion of "self expression" is considered crucial. We are encouraged to do our own thing, let it all hang out, and follow our instincts. This is a distortion of what we are taught in the Bible. We are not called to serve our own interests, but Christ's. In serving him comes real satisfaction, and a sense of purpose that the non-believer vainly struggles to discover. We mustn't be self-satisfied about our salvation, either. We are called not to judge, but to proclaim.

An art which develops from these principles will be healthy, even if not automatically brilliant. It won't be self-possessed or aloof. In all of the scale and majesty of God's universe and action, our artworks are really not very important. They are small, paltry things. Yet in another sense they are more important than we can ever realize. As our gifts are returned to God with the interest accrued through our use, they have a heavenly value — the value of God's acceptance and pleasure. Making an artwork can be a peaceful, absorbing activity with opportunity for reflection and meditation. As you work, think about the loving, creative God who has called you and given you his name. Reflect on the fact that Christ has made it possible for you to stand in the presence of God despite your failings, and that when rendered to the Creator all of our humble work has meaning. Picture it!

Appendix

An arts day (see page 112)

The following programme can be adapted to fit in with your local needs and resources. N.B. Each time-slot is given various possible activities. Your programme would have only one, unless it is planned for more than one hundred people!

Ensure plenty of opportunity for working in small groups, preferably with a plenary session at the end, so people can compare notes.

If you are very efficient you can appoint someone to write a follow-up letter thanking people for attending, and summarizing some of the discussion. This will make a second arts day even better attended.

10.00 a.m.
Coffee and welcome. Guests have been requested to bring work with them. They are asked at this time to put their work up on the walls before lunch.

10.30 a.m.
Bible study

12.00
An arts talk.

As this is just before lunch, it should be "light". Allow some time for questions, either in the course of the talk or at the end. Some indication of the type of thing you might want to put on:

■ An artist showing slides of his work and talking about his sketching-tour of Burkina Faso, his cold garret, and other fascinating experiences . . .

■ What is design? A talk about the visual properties of the common objects which surround us, tracing some key periods in the history of design, and discussing the relation between form, purpose, and style.

■ The serious cartoon. A cartoonist, or fan of cartoons, explains how the political cartoon originated and how it works. Illustrated.

■ A meditation on Psalm 19.1–6, which reflects on God's glory in creation.

■ An exploration of the work of the skilled craftsmen in creating the temple furnishings and clothes in Exodus 28.1–13 and 31.1–11.

■ A small group Bible study on either of the above subjects.

N.B. If you invite a speaker in to assist in the Bible study ensure they are told about the whole programme, and your goals for this session and for the whole day.

1.00 — 2.30 p.m.

This long lunch-break allows time for the artists who have come to put their work on the walls and for everyone to see it. Make sure that name tags are used to enable people to identify artworks with artists. At 2.30 call everyone together, and spend half-an-hour discussing works as a group. Let people ask the artists questions directly, or alternatively, ask to have questions submitted in writing. The latter will produce more penetrating questions, and helps to get the session off to a good start.

3.00 p.m.

Work-groups

Divide into groups, distribute paper and pencils. Ask each group to appoint one person to be a "leader" and play some of the drawing games (page 18). Then move on to one of the following possible assignments:

■ Design a poster to encourage people to help the poor
■ Design a poster on one of the Ten Commandments

Criticism

It is valuable to hone your critical faculties so that you question your own responses. When assessing an artwork produced by someone you know, remember that tact and graciousness are more likely to assist communication than are bluntness or waffling. Praise what is good before pointing out weakness. If you are being criticized, don't immediately erect electrified fences. Look at it this way: you are far more likely to learn something useful from negative comments than you are from being patted on the back. We all need some reassurance from time to time, but don't always insist on it, or you will stagnate.

116

■ Make some suggestions for the decoration of a church hall for one of the following: a children's summer mission, Lent, Christmas, Easter, a harvest festival, an overseas mission conference.

This session should be followed by a brief report from each of the group spokespersons. At the beginning of the session be sure to emphasize that it is not expected that a group will produce slick, finished designs. Rather, the purpose of the group session is to stimulate creative interactive thinking. The results of this short time spent together will extend beyond the arts day, for people will go away with their minds ticking over with ideas for expressing aspects of the Christian faith in visual form.

Indexes

Index of Bible references

This index lists all Bible passages and verses mentioned in this book.

Index of Technical tips. . .

Index of projects, games, activities, and worked examples

The following table lists all the projects described in *Picture It!* and suggests whether they are most useful for children's work, youth work, or adult church activities. ■ indicates the project is ideal for the age group. □ indicates it could be used with care or adaptation.

	Page	Children's work	Youth work	Adults
Animated film				
Using plasticine	103		■	■
Using people	104		■	■
Using puppets	104		■	■
Arts day	115			■
Backdrops	60	□	■	□
Banners	55			■
Cartoons	106		■	
Christmas cards	96		□	■
Collage	95	■	□	■
Drawing games:				
Absent objects	23		■	■
Contour lines	20		□	■
Emotions	23		■	■
Emotional shapes	25			■
Eye-shift	22			■
Heads up!	19		■	■
Object and environment	24		□	■
The drawing game	27		□	■
X-Ray vision	21			■
8mm film (animated film)				■
Games	108	■	■	■
Graffiti	105	□	■	■
Greeting cards	96		□	■
Hand-made books	101	□		■
Maps	108	■		■
Marbling paper	94	□	□	■
Masks	35	■		
Models:				
"Noah's ark"	107	■		
"Tabernacle" or "Sacred tent"	109	■		
Mural	64	■	■	□
Posters	81		□	■
Props	33	■		

120

New in the Creative Handbook Series

Everyone's a Winner
by Jim Belben and Trevor Cooper

The fruit of eight years extensive exploration on how games can be used to explore the Bible. It contains thirteen practical, thoroughly-tested games, role-plays, and simulations to explore the Bible. Some of the subjects covered are: boy-girl relationships, money, Old Testament relationship to New Testament, how we got our Bible, what should the church be doing, how do we make decisions, and much much more.

Other creative resources from Bible Society

1. *Pictures from the Gospels*
2. *Pictures from the Old Testament*

Two volumes of *Good News Bible* drawings ready to use on the overhead projector.

Modern translations of the Bible throughout the world have featured the illustrations of Swiss artist Annie Vallotton. In the *Good News Bible* she shows how a few simple lines can convey so much meaning to a very wide age-range.

Pictures from the Gospels and *Pictures from the Old Testament* make a selection of these, (plus some previously unpublished drawings) available on overhead projector acetates.

Particularly useful for family services, children's work and school assemblies, they can also be used to create the talking point which opens up discussion at a Bible study group.

Using the Bible in Drama
by Steve and Janet Stickley and Jim Belben

Now established as a standard work on the subject of starting a church drama group. It presents for free performance some of Footprints Theatre Company's most famous sketches and also includes advice on warming up, studying the Bible, writing through improvisation, performing and presenting your sketches.

Move Yourselves
by Gordon and Ronni Lamont

Eleven movement, mime, and dance workshops. Including four original performance pieces for the church festivals of Christmas, Easter, Pentecost, and Harvest. Written out of the vast workshop experience of the leaders and founders of Kinetik Theatre, Gordon and Ronni Lamont.

Show Me!
by Judy Gattis Smith

Fifteen techniques — and thirty ready-to-use examples — revealing how to use drama with children aged 3–13. Judy Gattis Smith wrote this book while a Director of Christian Education in a church in Williamsburg, Virginia, U.S.A. It was then tested, revised, and republished for use in the U.K.

Sketches/Notes

Sketches/Notes

Sketches/Notes

Sketches/Notes

Sketches/Notes

Sketches/Notes